Audience of One

My Story: From a Slave to Sin to Free in Christ and Everything in Between

TRISHA DAHLHEIMER

WESTBOW
PRESS®
A DIVISION OF THOMAS NELSON
& ZONDERVAN

WestBow Press books may be ordered through booksellers or by contacting:

WestBow Press
A Division of Thomas Nelson & Zondervan
1663 Liberty Drive
Bloomington, IN 47403
www.westbowpress.com
1 (866) 928-1240

Unless otherwise cited, scripture quotations taken from the New American Standard Bible® (NASB), Copyright © 1960, 1962, 1963, 1968, 1971, 1972, 1973, 1975, 1977, 1995 by The Lockman Foundation Used by permission. www.Lockman.org

Scripture quotations are from the ESV® Bible (The Holy Bible, English Standard Version®), copyright © 2001 by Crossway, a publishing ministry of Good News Publishers. Used by permission. All rights reserved.

Scripture quotations marked MSG are taken from THE MESSAGE, copyright © 1993, 2002, 2018 by Eugene H. Peterson. Used by permission of NavPress. All rights reserved. Represented by Tyndale House Publishers, Inc.

ISBN: 978-1-9736-7768-0 (sc)
ISBN: 978-1-9736-7770-3 (hc)
ISBN: 978-1-9736-7769-7 (e)

Library of Congress Control Number: 2019916736

Print information available on the last page.

WestBow Press rev. date: 11/1/2019

Dedicated to my Jesus. I would not have
done any of this without You.

Acknowledgments

Thank you to all the people who helped make this book a reality.

My girlfriends, you *all* have been the greatest cheerleaders a girl could have! Thank you for your listening ears, your advice on ideas, prayers during the tears, and praises. Thank you for the endless Bible studies and front-porch meetings, which contributed to a lot of this book. The laughs, too many to count, have been life giving.

My mentor and friend Janine, your wisdom on how to study the Bible was literally a godsend. Our countless hours at Starbucks and endless classes on the floor of the living room have breathed life into my soul. God used you in a mighty way to show me I could not only study the Bible on my own but also teach others.

Darren and Michaela, you are forever in my debt. Coffee is always on me!

My mom, thank you for your encouragement and kind words. This was some hard stuff, and I know I broke your heart a few times in the process. You are the best woman I know, and I am so proud to be your daughter.

My kids, thank you for the days you gave me in the office. Thank you for picking up the slack and making dinners, cleaning the house, and just altogether being amazing kids. You are rock stars!

Finally, my husband, Nate—Natey Cakes, My Moon and My Stars—you have supported me through many, many things.

We have been through a lot, but all situations have led me to love you more. You are a rock and my love. You bring me down when I am flying high, and you have and will continue to leap with me on countless adventures. Thank you for being my tentmaker and supporting me so I can follow the path God has set before me. I am a better woman, mom, speaker, and writer because of you.

Contents

Foreshadow

I wonder if anyone knows I'm under here? she thought. Her secret place was under the kitchen counter. She was still young enough and short enough to stand there and not touch the countertop with her head. Adults couldn't do that, and her brother couldn't anymore either. So it was her special place. She would hide there when she played hide-and-seek. It was the same counter where she ate her breakfast very morning.

This day she was all alone. No one was in the room with her, and no one was looking for her. It seemed to her that she had been under there for a long time, and no one even noticed. Her mom walked into the room and made a phone call. Focused on the call she was making, her mother never looked in the little girl's direction. The girl knew her mom didn't notice her because she had her eyes on her mom the whole time.

Boy, she seems happy to talk to whoever she called, the girl thought. Her mom was talking and laughing, engrossed in her conversation with her friend.

Suddenly, her dad came stomping into the room. He also didn't notice her under the counter. *Wow, this is a good hiding spot,* she thought. But then she saw her dad was mad. Her mom's laughter stopped immediately, and she hung up the phone. She wasn't happy anymore; in fact, she started to cry.

Why is Dad so mad? she wondered. His face was red with rage, blame, painful love, all bursting forth. She wasn't worried that her dad would hurt her mom, but she could see he was enraged and hurt deeply. Her mom looked exhausted, almost like she had nothing left to give. She was broken and unwilling to be fixed.

Seeing the hurt and pain manifested in her parents, the girl started to whimper softly enough to herself that she remained unseen and unheard. She heard a dark voice in her head. *They are going to leave you! You will never be enough. You will always be alone.*

She thought, *Why has no one noticed* me? No one even *looked* for her. Did no one *care* about her? Was she really all alone? Maybe the voice was right. *I'm not good enough, and no one wants me anymore.*

Her eyes burned from staring. Her head ached from trying to understand what was happening. *Why is no one noticing me here? Why do I feel so alone? These people are my rocks. What is happening? I'm scared.*

She was alone, or was she?

Her audience of One was right there with her, but it would take years for her to be able to see Him.

Audience of One:
Long List of Credentials

Trisha Dahlheimer
Born.

Thirty-three years passed…

Born again.

These are my credentials. They are what I have to bring to this table. So this is me, holding out my arms and saying, "Here I am, Lord. Pick me!" My hope for this book is that you won't just see me but that instead you will see Jesus through me.

In the book of Exodus, there is a conversation between Moses and God. God was giving Moses a rundown on the call He had put on Moses's life. God told Moses what He wanted Moses to do with his life. Can you imagine? Moses got a firsthand account from the God of the universe on what His purpose for his life was. When God told Moses he was to free the Israelites, Moses replied, "Please, Lord, I have never been eloquent, either recently or in the past, nor since you have spoken to me, your servant; for I am slow of speech and slow of tongue."[1] Why would Moses question God? Right before I studied Exodus this morning, I asked God,

---

[1] Exodus 4:10 NASB

"Really, Lord, You want *me* to write a book? I barely graduated from high school." I was known for being a terrible speller. I shared an apartment with two of my best friends. We split the expenses, and I was in charge of the cable bill. Every month I wrote a huge note on the refrigerator, listing what each person owed me. "CABEL $17.56 each." That's what my spelling was like then. I became a hairstylist because, thank God, I could do that well. "Then, Lord, You took me out of the salon two weeks after I give my life to You." What? The one thing I did well? Other than doing hair, I never really did anything well. But I didn't even think twice about quitting once I got a glimpse of You. But a book? Rant over.

So that was my "convo" with God, and *then* I read how Moses had reacted to his call. What was Moses thinking? He questioned God? Oh, no, you didn't Moses! Oh, yes, you did! I guess I'm not so different from this man of the Bible. I actually found myself all over the Bible. More on that later. All that to say

I bring you my credentials.

Born.
Thirty-three years ...
Born again.

Moses's conversation with God continues in Exodus 4:11. "The Lord says, 'Who has made man's mouth? Or who makes him mute or deaf or seeing or blind? Now then GO and I, *even I* will be with your mouth, and teach you what you are to say.' Then Moses says, 'Please Lord now send the message by whomever You will [but not me, Lord]!'" (emphasis added). "The Lord grew angry with Moses and said, 'Your brother Aaron, can do it.'" What God was saying was, "Aaron does speak fluently, but I wanted you, Moses." And that is what happened. Aaron spoke for Moses.

This story makes me so sad. God knew Aaron was a better

speaker. God wasn't surprised by this fact. But He wanted Moses, even though he wasn't the most eloquent speaker. *But God wanted him!* I wonder how the story would have been different if Moses had trusted God with his slow speech.

What if God has something planned for us, but we cannot understand? What if I look around and see so many people who are far more qualified to do what He has called me to do? Am I the most qualified? No. Am I the only one who is up for this task? Certainly not. In fact, I am quite ill equipped, weak, and weary over Your call on my life, God. But I will look You in the face and follow You and You alone. Moses collapsed in the face of adversity.

Not everyone shied away so easily from God's calling on his or her life. Some dropped everything and followed Him. One day Jesus had just started His ministry and began to have a following. So many people wanted to hear His teaching that He decided to go out in a boat and teach the people from there. When He finished teaching, He told one of the fishermen to let his nets back out into the deep. "And Simon Peter answered, 'Master, we toiled all night and took nothing! But at your word I will let down the nets'" (Luke 5:5).

Sure enough, their obedience paid off. The nets were full to the point that when they pulled them into the boat, the boat started to sink. I love Peter's response. "But when Simon Peter saw it, he fell down to Jesus' knees, saying, 'Depart from me, for I am a sinful man O, Lord'" (Luke 5:8).

Can you imagine this scene? Simon Peter jumped out of the sinking boat, ran through the water as fast as he could, then splashed down at Jesus's feet. Soaked to the bone, hair dripping wet, he choked on the water and his words. "Lord, how can this be that You are here for me? How are You here with me? I am so unworthy."

Simon Peter isn't the only one who saw what Jesus did and changed his or her life because of it. Peter's fishing partners, James and John, saw and were scared. Jesus said, "'Do not be afraid; from now on you will be catching men.' And when they had brought their boats to land, they left everything and followed him" (Luke 5:10–11).

I will drop everything and follow You. But God, You have called me to something outside my wheelhouse, and I need You to be my mouth and continue to teach me what to say. This is Your testimony of Your love and grace. Use my fingers to show the world that You can love this broken, approval-seeking, overeating, comfort-seeking, prideful, cracked human being, who has fallen desperately in love with You.

Introduction

I'm trying to keep myself together,
to keep myself sane through all of this,
but there are moments when
I am completely losing my mind.

—Unknown

Does anyone else feel as if you are constantly spinning your wheels? That life is a constant struggle to dance through? That your only objective is not to fall and knock everyone over in your path? Like making everyone happy is an exhausting task only a superhero could possibly handle? Being a wife and mother, I think I should have been given superpowers. I should have been given a little something extra to get through each day.

These people want to eat. Every. Single. Day. Three times a day! I, for one, really don't enjoy cooking. I'm pretty sure my husband thought that when we got married fifteen years ago that I would magically love cooking and cleaning. That the married gene would kick in and that I would become an amazing chef and housekeeper. FYI, that didn't happen. I fumbled along with my George Foreman and Pledge, trying to make our house a home. Anyone? Yes, of course, there will be some of you reading who have no idea what I'm talking about. The gifted women have it all together; they love cooking and cleaning, the Monica Gellers of the world. But stick with me; there might even be something for you here too.

I was also a full-time hairstylist, trying to build a clientele and manage a salon of twenty women. By the way, they were all older than I. At that time, I thought I was juggling a lot of balls high up in the air.

Now it's fifteen years later. Add in three kids, house number six, homeschooling, and running multiple businesses. And I'm still trying to be attractive for my husband while spinning my wheels!

Again, to be honest, I feel extremely inadequate to be doing *anything* like this, *but* here I am—pen to paper or fingers to keyboard, writing a book.

In these pages I am praying you will see that life doesn't need to be like this. Life isn't meant to be a series of painful days of not being enough and being a disappointment to everyone around you. I pray you will see that there is Someone out there who wants to carry your burdens and guide you through this life. This is a Person who wants to light the path before you. He walked the very path He is asking you to walk. He softens the blow of hard news just with His presence.

When spring comes to this great state of Minnesota, everyone goes outside. My mornings change from the office inside to the couch on the porch. I spend my time reading and studying with the sound of birds singing and deer walking through the front yard. But my dogs need to learn again how *not* to run after every person who walks by with his or her dog. Often I am reading or writing and smiling to myself. How much I love spring mornings on the porch, when out of the blue come an eruption of barking, claws digging into the slippery deck, and pain in my ears. I'm shocked out of my peaceful morning. The dogs are on the attack.

Mind you, we have a friendly lab named Maggie. If anyone turns in her direction, she either wags her tail or runs in the other direction. Then we have a Yorkie named Jasper, who thinks he is a pit bull. Neither would do any harm; nevertheless, I have to run down the driveway after them, often in my pajamas. I apologize for my dogs as I run down to the street, hoping the passerby doesn't look in my direction. Humiliating. Makes me dislike having animals. Why can't they just sit on the porch with me and enjoy watching the birds, deer, people, and dogs casually walking by?

Yesterday, Nate was with me on the porch. It was a beautiful morning. All the wonders of nature were around us. The birds were singing, the wind chimes singing ever so softly. The morning was so beautiful that the neighbors were also out walking. No one said a thing; we just sat and took in the beauty. Suddenly, I realized both dogs were on the porch with us; it took me a minute to take it all in. I started thinking, *why are the dogs just sitting just sitting and looking at the dogs walking by with their owners? Was this really happening? Why weren't they barking and running? Why were they staying and just watching? Were all my dreams coming true? Had I finally trained them to sit and stay? Were my wild animals now free to stay out here with me every day without risk of incident and punishment?*

Then I looked over and saw my big, strong husband sitting next me and enjoying the morning as much as I was. Then I realized something; it was *his* presence that made the dogs behave. It was just him sitting silently on the porch that made the dogs act so differently. He didn't say a word to them to make them obey; he was just *there*, in their presence.

Why? Was this due to fear? The dogs didn't seem afraid. Or did they *know* he would protect me so they didn't have to? They didn't have to stand up for me; there was someone stronger and more powerful sitting there, ready to protect their mama at a moment's notice. With him there, fear was gone, peace reigned, and all things fell into place.

He was enough.

That is how we should relate to God. *His* presence is enough to give us peace, take away fear, and cause us to do what is right. That dancing through this life for Him and Him alone is *enough*! He truly is your only audience.

I heard a story once about a group of siblings who put a play together for their mom. They worked all day on this riveting performance, and they couldn't wait to show their audience, but when they called their mom in to witness this gem, they set out the one chair for the audience to sit in and announced something like this. "We would like to thank our 'audient' for coming today!" She was their only hearer, the only person for them to perform for. She was their "audient."

Who is your "audient"? Whom are you performing for? Who is listening to your every word? Who is delighted in your performances? Let me tell you about my journey when I met my "audient."

CHAPTER 1

How Could This "Happen" to Me?

If you look at the world, you'll be distressed.
If you look within, you'll be depressed.
But if you look at Christ, You'll be at rest.
—Corrie ten Boom

My parents divorced when I was six years old. Life was like that of most American children with divorced parents. We had the every-other-weekend thing, the stepparent thing, the stepsisters and stepbrother thing. We all had our ups and downs, but mostly life was good from my perspective as a child.

Mom was always gracious and caring; she never said a bad word about our dad. Frankly, I don't remember her saying anything bad about anyone. Unfortunately, Dad didn't share the same standard. He made comments and jokes in front of us. This didn't happen often, not always, but it was enough that I remember it. Thankfully it never made me think bad about Mom; it actually made me see a sadness in my dad. Even at my young age, I could see it. Now, an outsider probably wouldn't recognize it, but there is something about divorce that just wounds so many people in its wake. Most of the destruction is unseen to the naked eye, but to the wounded, it is always there, even if we don't know it or admit it.

Our weekends with Dad were filled with camping, fishing,

roller coasters, and rides. Basically, at Dad's we were sure to have the time of our lives, and at Mom's life was filled with strict rules and schedules. Both parents we loved. Although my mom never said anything to us kids, I'm sure she hated the fact that she had to have discipline and order and that Dad was "fun Dad."

So when "Fun Dad" got remarried years later and moved to a lake about forty minutes away, my brother, Matt, and I thought we would love to live there permanently. No strict rules and fun all the time. Every teenager's dream, right? Somehow my mother allowed this move to happen. I don't remember her fighting it, but I remember exactly what she was wearing and the look on her face when we drove away to move to Dad's. She told me later it was like we had died.

Gut punch as a mom now.

During this first fourteen years of my life, I believe, I learned a life-changing lesson: not all lessons are good or even true. But the lesson I learned was that I needed a savior. Not a Savior, capital S, but what I thought a savior was, a man to save me. If you want to be safe and protected, find a guy, and he will do and be all you need. When Mom and Dad got a divorce, we had my mom's boyfriend, Mike, who would come and buy us extravagant gifts. He was so nice to us.

Mike didn't last very long. Then there was Rocky. He literally came and saved us when our house was broken into, and he let us live with him. Not only did Rocky have a large dog that made us feel safe, but he also lived up to his name. Rocky looked just like Sylvester Stallone. He had the tan skin, dark hair, and big black mustache—and of course the huge muscles.

I remember one day when my mom and Rocky came home. Mom was all dressed up in a dress suit of sorts, and I don't remember what he was wearing, but they both had excited looks on their faces. It was the look you have when you have a wonderful surprise for someone, like the time when you find out last minute that you're going camping or you hear a snow day announcement.

This surprise wasn't like that at all. Mom came to my brother and me, and told us they had gotten married ... What?

Now, her then husband wasn't a bad guy; in fact, I really liked him. He was a savior of sorts for us. Still, on the day they sprang the marriage on us, I cried. Cried like I never remember crying before. My dad, my "real" father, was supposed to be my protector and my live-in savior, not this replacement. In the back of my mind, I had always thought my mom and dad would get back together. Now that dream was shattered.

Another twenty-five years would pass before I met my heavenly Father, the One who will never leave me or forsake me. The One who is all-knowing and ever present. The One who would unlock my heart to love and be loved. For the next twenty-five years, I toiled and toiled to be a good person so I could earn such a love, only to find out I could never be good enough or work hard enough.

So in the meantime I depended on my brother, Matt, to be my all and all. After all, he was always there; whichever house we were visiting, Matt was there with me. Plus his personality is one that will always allow me to be exactly who I am at all times. He has always supported me and loved me right where I am. He has been my rock.

Okay, where was I? ... Oh yeah, we moved to Dad's house right before freshman year.

Shortly after we moved to "Fun Dads," I met a guy. He was amazing. He was on the football team and the basketball team; he was very handsome and *very* confident, I thought. I was amazed that he wanted to date *me*. I was very plain; I didn't really wear makeup or have any real fashion sense. I look back on the pictures and think, *What was I thinking?* But honestly I didn't put much thought into how I looked. On the day I asked this guy out on a date—yes, *I* asked *him*—I wore bib overalls with a gingham green and white, sweetheart neckline, *bodysuit* under it. Boom! I was hot! Ha-ha! Ooh, how things changed ...

My dad called our family "E and C Christians" (Easter and Christmas). We darkened the door of a church on those two holidays. The rest of the year we were "fine." Now, our parents made sure we were baptized as infants, had godparents, and took our first communions; but they never talked about a relationship with Christ. They could give to us only what they had, and what they had were religious boxes to be checked in their book of parenting 101.

Baptize, check.

First communion, check.

Good people, check.

Although we didn't attend church regularly, I still had the knowledge of right and wrong. Two of the convictions I had were that abortions were bad and so were people who have sex before marriage.

So, much to our surprise, a few months into my junior year, I became pregnant.

At first my response was shock. How could this have happened to me? I was a "good person." I literally thought that being a "good" person would somehow stop this bad thing from happening to me. Clearly no one had sat down and explained the birds and the bees to me, but actually someone did. To my horror, our dad sat my brother and me down one weekend with a book. It had cartoonlike pictures explaining the entire process. Just what every girl wants to do with her weekend. Learn about sex with her older brother and her dad. *Ew.* Even with that gross attempt at informing me about the truths of sex and pregnancy, I didn't learn. I was blindsided.

I wish I would have known "all turned aside; together they have become corrupt; there is no one who is good, not even one" (Psalm 14:3). But it would be years before I would learn this.

My boyfriend, Joe, wanted me to have an abortion. Now remember that an abortion was on the list of things I would *never* do. But I found myself sitting in an abortion clinic with Joe's dad and girlfriend, trying to figure out how we were going to pay for this so I could keep the abortion from my parents. Don't judge me! Well, I'm sure you already did, which is fine, but this situation proved to me that I would have no business judging what I would do in one situation or another until I was in that very situation.

Here I was, doing what I had said I would never do. I left that appointment feeling relieved that I had a way to hide my shame. During the weeks ahead, I didn't have much to do. I just had to go back to the clinic for a consultation; then I would be all set. The day of the consultation came, but my boyfriend said he couldn't go with me and miss school because he had skipped too much already. *Really? You're going to make me do this by myself?* I for one *never* skipped school. I would have been terrified. Remember, I was a good person.

So I showed up at the house of a male friend and asked him to come with me. I have no idea why I picked him, probably because I was hiding the pregnancy from all my girlfriends and knew they wouldn't let me have an abortion. But Mike was supportive and said he would come along. He didn't mind skipping school. We had no idea where this place was. I had already been there but apparently wasn't paying attention. We got terribly lost. I called my boyfriend for help with the directions, and to my surprise he was at home. *What?* I was devastated. So I was crying, a complete mess; all the hopes and dreams I had seemed to be fading away with each step. I'm sure my poor sixteen-year-old male friend was having the time of his life. Could you imagine?

We arrived at the clinic too late for my appointment, and they sent us away. So I went back to school to catch the wrestling match, since I was a cheerleader. I finished off the day like a typical sixteen-year-old girl. Unbeknownst to the people around me, I was drowning.

This savior I thought would protect me and be there for me and comfort me had failed.

On the day I skipped school, my dad showed up to get my

report card. Because my grades were less than stellar, I purposely didn't bring my report card home. Now, during this time my grades plummeted, as you can imagine, so I wasn't going to bring the proof home. I found out later that my dad had asked Matt, my brother, what he thought my problem was. Was I on drugs or pregnant? Matt said, "Well, she's definitely not pregnant. She would never do that." I had everyone fooled. Well, not anymore.

I told my dad I was pregnant but that I'd tried to get an abortion so they wouldn't find out. The desire for an abortion vanished the moment my pregnancy was brought to light. But the battle was far from over. My dad softened immediately; he showed me great compassion and gentleness in the situation. He had no answers for me at that point but told me I needed to tell my mom. Mom was sad at first; she had also gone through some major life changes during this time. She had learned her husband, Rocky, was unfaithful many times, and he ended up leaving their marriage. Around this time she decided to accept Christ as her Savior and Lord of her life. She then wanted to talk about Jesus all the time, but I just tuned her out. I had no interest in a boring life with God. By the end of this particular conversation about being pregnant, she was picking out baby names and excited to have her first grandbaby.

Well, now both of my parents knew my secret. What was next?

CHAPTER 2

Out of Denial and into the Nile

Pharaoh commanded all his people,
"Every son that is born to the Hebrews,
you shall cast into the Nile, but you
shall let every daughter live."

—Exodus 1:16

After the dust and shock settled, all the opinions started to surface. What should I do about this baby? My boyfriend still held onto the abortion option, but by this time our relationship had pretty much ended. I don't even know whether we ever had a conversation about ending it. I just wanted my family, and he was—let's face it—a seventeen-year-old boy. How on earth was he going to be expected to handle this? I, on the other hand, had no choice. "Handle it," I must.

But what in the world? I had found a guy! Why hadn't I been saved? I thought having a guy would make all my dreams comes true, right? Shouldn't I have been dreaming of a wedding and a perfect life ahead of me? The fairy-tale life? Mine looked much different from any fairy tale I had read.

I guess I was on my own. I *had* to deal with it. My dad, I learned much later, called a meeting with his siblings right before Christmas to discuss and decide what Trisha should do. Thank You, Jesus, that I was in the dark about this meeting. I went to

Christmas dinner totally naive to the fact that everyone knew of my shame. I would have been devastated and kind of still was once I learned about it. But anyway, they decided I needed to keep the baby.

So my boyfriend wanted the abortion. Dad and his family were team keep baby. Dad even thought I should let him and his then wife raise the baby for the first five years. See, they didn't have any kids together, so Dad thought this was a win win. His wife got a baby for a few years, and I could still finish school and go to college. Then I would take my baby back. You might need a minute to play that whole situation out in your head. Oh, and did I mention the fact that I also didn't get along with my stepmom?

Lord, please don't ever call my children to write a story about their lives with me as their mom. I have made so many mistakes in parenting and so forth. My parents did the best they could, and I love them so much for sticking by me through all my ups and downs in life. Please don't see the actions of my parents as mistakes but as me being molded and shaped into the woman God has made me today. Cracks and scars and all.

Anyway, so what did Mom think? Through continued prayer, she came to the conclusion that adoption was the best option. My brother, my other most important opinion holder in my life, proved to be once again the supportive brother without an opinion. Which was a breath of fresh air.

My head was spinning. Everywhere I turned, someone had another opinion. Abortion? Adoption? Keep the baby? Or even lend him out for a few years. Yes, I did find out by this time that I was having a boy. I thought knowing would help my decision process somehow, but it didn't.

I finally asked everyone to keep his or her opinions to himself or herself. I needed to make this choice for myself and the baby. The next few months were a blur.

Not only do I relate with Moses, but I really relate to his mother. She also had a terrible decision set before her.

Exodus 1 explains that a new king arose in Egypt, one who didn't know Joseph. He didn't know all the amazing things Joseph had done for Egypt. All the new king could see was that the Hebrew people were growing into huge numbers. They were so large that if they, the Hebrews, saw war come against Egypt, they might fight for the other nation and overtake Egypt. His solution was to make them slaves and become lord over them. Why would he do this? Why not align with the Hebrews or band together? I don't know, I guess. I'm not a king, so maybe if I were, I would come to that conclusion. His plan backfired. The more he oppressed them, the more they multiplied.

Solution number one was to order all the midwives, *Hebrew* midwives, to kill the *Hebrew* baby boys and let the baby girls live. Huh? What was he thinking? He told women to kill babies. He told *Hebrew* women to kill *Hebrew* babies. Did he know nothing about women and babies? Had he never seen women with babies? Did he not have a sister, wife, or daughter? How could he think this was a good plan? "But the midwives feared God and did not do as the king commanded them, but let the male children live" (Exodus 1:17).

They chose not to abort the babies, but they let them live. Yay, God-fearing midwives! Reading this in black and white makes it seem like such an easy decision. Of course, you wouldn't do that, right? That's your own people, Hebrew midwives. Of course that was a no-brainer, right? Or was it? They would have risked their lives *not* to kill these babies. They would have been brought before the king and have to answer for not doing what he had commanded. God gave them an out for this excruciating decision.

The king did bring them forward, "He said, 'Why have you done this thing, and let the boys live?' The Hebrew midwives said to Pharaoh, 'Because the Hebrew women are not as the Egyptian women: for they are vigorous and give birth before the midwife could get to them.'"

Finally, out of amazing frustration, I'm sure, King Pharaoh

ordered his own people, Egyptian soldiers, to kill the baby boys, saying, "Every son who is born to the Hebrews you are to cast into the Nile, and every daughter you are to keep alive" (Ex. 1:22).

Solution number two: The king demanded that his own people kill the babies in the Nile River after they were born. They were supposed to throw them in and watch them drown. That step is hard for me to swallow. Notice that he never did anything himself. He always ordered other people to do these horrific acts. He never once said, "Okay, if you're not going to do this, I will come down there and do this myself." Never did he say that. Now I know he was king and all, and it was his job to delegate, but I would have liked to see him try to do these terrible things himself, which he was putting on others.

Moses's mom was named Jochebed. That's a name you don't hear every day. I wonder what her mom thought when she was born. *Oh, baby girl Jochebed … perfect!* Anyway … Jochebed gave birth to Moses, and she saw he was beautiful, so she hid him for three months.

How was he more beautiful than any other baby? Would she not have hidden him if he had been unfortunate looking? I did have another baby boy years and years later. When he was born, the cord was wrapped around his neck four times … yep, *four* times. The moment the baby was born and safe, my poor doctor ran out of the room. I'm sure she went to go cry somewhere. I was none the wiser. My husband said he saw the look on her face when she said it was wrapped around yet another time. He said he was ready to hip check her out of the way and pull that baby out. I thankfully had no idea there was a potential problem.

He was, or appeared to be, perfectly healthy. But then we looked at him … he was all battered and swollen. His poor little eyes were so swollen that we could barely see what color his eyes were. I remember thinking, *Is this what he will always look like?* I mean, this wasn't my first rodeo; he was actually my third baby, but none of them had looked like this. Later, both Nate and I admitted we were a little scared to show this baby off to our family; he looked really rough for about three days. Now, of course, he's the cutest boy anyone ever could lay eyes on. But I'm sure glad I didn't have to decide based on his beauty whether we were going to keep him.

Thankfully, the word *beautiful* used here is the word *towb* in Hebrew. It is the same word God used to describe His creation. He saw what He had created, and it was *towb*. He created man and female, and He saw they were very *towb*. Moses's mom saw Moses, and he was *towb*. So she hid him for three months. She hid his cries from the guards. She hid all evidence of a baby living in her house. Let me ask those of you who have babies or know someone who has one a question. What happens to your house when the tiny human enters? It's equivalent to a bomb going off, with baby things everywhere. Now, during Moses's time, they didn't have rooms decorated months before the blessed baby came, bottles and disposable diapers, or contraptions you could hang from your doorways for the baby to bounce in, but I'm sure there were still things to hide—dirty laundry and baby *smells*—but she did this for three months until the situation became too hard, and she made a decision.

She mapped out her baby's best chance for survival and executed it at just the right time. She placed her baby in a wicker basket. This word *basket* in the text is actually better translated as *ark*. It is the same word used for Noah's ark—you know, the one who saved all of mankind and animal kind from the earth's flood? Jochebed placed Moses in his "ark" in her last-ditch effort to save her baby, to give him a fighting chance.

That is the same decision I made. I decided on my own to give him (my baby) up for adoption. It was my final-ditch effort to give this baby boy a fighting chance, a chance to have a mother and a father, a chance to have siblings close to his age.[2] I wanted

---

[2] He did in fact end up with a brother and a sister close to his age. Yeah, God!

him to have a chance to grow up in a home without separation and moving, and to have the stability I had always longed for.

So I placed him in an ark and put him in the Nile, hoping and praying he would be better because of my sacrifice; that his life wouldn't be filled with moving back and forth from parent to parent every other weekend. He wouldn't need to go on an endless search for safety and security. He wouldn't need to wonder whether Mom was coming home or Dad would be able to get out of his robe or stepparent number "?" would stick around. He could float through life and find his own savior to scoop him up and *love* him!

By the grace of God, I know all these things are true. He and his family live twenty-five minutes from us now. I stayed in contact with his mom all these years, and my family even attended his graduation. We got to meet his friends and extended family. I saw firsthand that he has an amazing family that loves him and has provided all the things I wished for him.

God is so amazing! When Moses's mom placed him in his ark, he floated to an unexpected place, straight into the arms of Pharaoh's daughter. He was saved by the very family that had set the course of his fatal trip down the Nile.

This gets me thinking … Is there a Nile I should be floating down? Is there an ark waiting for me? When the pressures come, does God have an ark built and ready for me to jump into? Or do I need to build my own ark? What about you?

Turns out I *was* a child in my own ark. I was a child with a child. My child got plucked out by an amazing God-fearing family, and they have loved and cared for him ever since. I, however, kept floating. Waves crashed, rapids raged, and I was in the ark, being tossed to and fro. My every situation determined how I felt. My every thought ruled my actions. I was on a wild ride with no rudder or steering wheel. Wherever the river of culture and peer pressure went, I went with it. I was a prisoner to the river and its waves, trapped in a culture I couldn't control, and I couldn't see the shore.

At the end of the Old Testament, God had spoken to so many people in so many ways; some of them we will talk about in this book. But at the end of the Old Testament, God went silent for four hundred years. Just like the Hebrew people were in slavery for four hundred years in Egypt, now His people entered the slavery of a silent God.

For many generations no one heard the voice of God. Not through a dream, a vision, a prophet, or even His word. He was silent. Then finally He broke the silence in a very unexpected way.

With a baby's cry.

Jesus's cry in that manger.

The reason we celebrate Christmas is because of the unexpected voice of God through a baby. God is so creative. I try and try to predict what He will do next, and He always surprises me. Jesus was born to a single mother, not yet married. She was young and scared like me. She was scared like Jochebed, Moses's mother. Why would God do that? Moses could have been born to anyone. He could have been born at any time. God could have decided he would be born to the most powerful, richest family on the planet. But no, he came as a humble servant to his people.

I don't think he grew up like I did, though. Let me tell you how I grew up.

CHAPTER 3

Stable Castles

I have come as Light into the world,
so that everyone who believes in me
will not remain in darkness.

—John 12:46

The rest of my teen years were pretty typical for an American teenager in the '90s. Mall bangs, sequined prom dresses, and the continuation of the "Who am I?" game. I was continuing to float along, looking for my audience. *Okay*, I thought, *let's try the "Let's try" game; let's try smoking cigarettes.* Okay, I liked smoking enough to do so for the next seven years. Let's try the weekend parties and alcohol. I loved this also. I held on to this lifestyle for a little longer than seven years. More like sixteen years of drinking and partying. Almost everything I did revolved around alcohol.

That fact seems strange for me to even admit. I wasn't the person who got drunk at work or added whiskey to my morning latte. I was the girl who thought that to be noticed I needed to be fun, spontaneous, silly; and that goal fit in really well at the bar. At the same time, I noticed the guys weren't lined up at the door to meet me. I wasn't the one everyone was setting up with his or her friends. I felt unseen in this way. I always blamed it on how I looked. I wasn't heavy, but I for sure wasn't the skinny girl at the party. So I always felt overlooked. You know what I mean? You

15

walk into a room full of men, and they see right through you. That was how I saw it, so alcohol would help me to be seen or not care that I wasn't. At the time I had no idea how it all was just feeding my insecurities. I thought drinking and smoking would help me to be fun, liked, and wanted.

When I think back on those years (and when I'm really honest with myself), those were the loneliest years of my life. Sure, I had a lot of friends and was rarely alone. But I always had an underlying need to perform for everyone. What everyone around me thought of me was the most important thing to me. Just being myself wasn't enough. Am I the only one who has ever felt this way? I can't be.

Right after high school, I went to beauty school. I went to learn how to cut and color hair and many other things like nails, skin care, makeup, perms, and so forth, but that wasn't all I learned in those months. I learned that *You better up your game, country girl, or you will drown!* This was my first experience in the city. I grew up about forty-five minutes from downtown, and wow, it was a whole different world—not just geographically. But it was also a new industry I was entering.

I went from my senior pictures with little to no makeup and no color in my hair to every different color you could think of in my hair and never leaving the house without a *lot* of makeup. My uncle likes to tell the story about the time I showed up to Christmas dinner with "Christmas red" hair. If that wasn't bad enough, I also had one side sticking straight out and the other side neatly lying down. His shock and horror were met with my sweet face and me not thinking there was anything off with my hairstyle choices. The fact that I had multiple piercings in my face may have gotten him too. Ha! True story.

Disclaimer: I still do love the fun, crazy, creative art of hair. But what I was doing wasn't art; it was a search for significance, a desperate attempt to be seen or wanted.

Over the years behind the chair, my hair tamed a bit, but my search for significance didn't slow down. I still thought I needed to have a man to save me or complete me. I wanted to show the world I was worthy to be loved, that I, too, was able to get someone to love me, protect me, see me. How is it that we can be surrounded by people and still feel unseen or unloved?

During this time a friend and I went to Cozumel for a vacation getaway. She and I had been friends for years, and our dating and breakups seemed to be totally in sync. We were both on a dry spell with boyfriends. So why not a vacation week in Mexico for two twentysomething girls? One of the nights we drank so much that we blacked out. When we got our pictures back, there was a picture of us on a barber's chair and in a locker room. I had a blue wig on ... huh? It is only by God's grace that we made it back to our hotel room unscathed.

The next day we were signed up for a trip to the mainland to go to an amazing tropical zoo. The ferry was *not* okay with me! The captain of the ship gave me a bag I could get sick in, but it was a clear plastic bag. Classy. So when we got off the boat, I had to walk through a town full of people, carrying my shame for everyone to see ... literally.

After a week of drinking and getting ourselves into some very unsafe situations, we both decided we needed to move to Cozumel. No joke. We put our money together and decided we could live there for about six months on our savings. I could do some hair braiding on the beaches to make some extra money. I do love braiding hair. Perfect! I mean, of course, this was a brilliant idea. Right?

About three weeks into our trip planning, my world turned upside down. Let me set the stage.

For any of you who haven't experienced northern Minnesota in February, that month in northern Minnesota is cold and snowy. But sixteen of my closest female relatives would plan a trip to the same town up north every year. This was the second year I was old enough to go. Once we got to town, we didn't have to think too hard about what to do. There wasn't a whole lot going on in this one-horse town. One of the bars we loved had a great DJ, so we got all dressed up and headed into town for a fun night of drinking and dancing. Our feet killed by the end of the night, and our faces hurt from all the laughing.

This time was a little different.

One of my cousins and I decided to play pool. I was never great at bar games, but I did enjoy trying. So I was whacking away at the balls when suddenly I looked across the bar and locked eyes with the most mesmerizing blue eyes I had ever seen. I mean, seriously this guy had *all* of his teeth; that fact may or may not have been rare in this town. He also had a shaved head, Sorel boots (untied) with his jeans tucked into them, and did I mention the piercing blue eyes? I know what you are thinking ... Wow, he had it all! Yep. As a bonus, every time I looked at him he had a different shirt on. Remember winters in Minnesota. He came in layers.

I had to meet this guy, obviously. As I watched him walk back to his friends, lightning struck. I knew one of his friends. What were the chances? I'm pretty sure I *ran* over to meet my Prince Charming. It ended up that his name was Nate, not Prince Charming, but nonetheless we were married eighteen months later.

This guy was going to be it! He listened to me when I spoke; he even seemed to be interested in what I was saying. Surely he would be my savior.

My savior he was in a lot of ways. Our lives settled down pretty fast. I quit smoking on our honeymoon. I know that could seem like a terrible idea, but it actually worked to be out of my routine. We built a house, and I was going to get the stability I had always wanted.

Nate recently reminded me of a time when we went to dinner with our parents, and apparently I started crying because I was telling them that all I wanted was stability. To me stability meant we would buy a house and live in it *forever*. That ideal is stability.

While I waited for this "stable castle" to be built, I put other expectations on Nate to make me feel good about myself. How I felt about myself depended on Nate. It depends on whether he told me I was pretty, skinny, or successful. *Then* I would have a great day. Of course, he didn't do that every day, so then it depended on whether I *felt* like he thought I was pretty, skinny, or successful; then it was a good day. He was the temperature gauge of my self-worth. Unbeknownst to him, I had hired him for that job and found out he wasn't very good at the job I'd secretly given him. He wasn't groomed for it.

I tried to teach him. I made sure to tell him when he didn't measure up to my secret expectations. I tried to tell him how to do things better. Most often we both left those conversations feeling hurt, alone, and confused. In Nate's defense he tried; he tried so hard to be enough for me. I adore him for his countless unsuccessful efforts to make me happy. I couldn't even see what I was doing to my husband, my marriage, and myself. I spent my time blaming Nate when he wasn't meant for the position I had put on him.

He is a gift from God. That is actually what *Nathan* means: gift from God. I was getting my *gift* confused with my *savior*. Nate was a beautiful gift given to me to be my partner, not my savior.

Moses also had meaning to his name. When he was old enough not to be nursed any longer, the word says his mother brought him to Pharaoh's daughter, and he became her son. She named him Moses because, she said, "I drew him out of the water" (Exodus 2:10). The words were very literal. *Moses* means "drawn from water."

The adopted parents of my son also named their boy Nathan. They said, "He is a gift from God." How crazy is that? When I was seventeen years old, I was given a gift I was able to give away. Then eight years later, I was given a gift to have and to hold.

Moses definitely wasn't counting blessings at this point. He was now ripped away from his mother and his people, and he found himself trading a cave for a castle. Moses was probably not weened until well into his toddler years. He would have known who his mother was, and he would have known the ways of the people. I don't know whether his mom told him he wouldn't always live with her or that his home would be in the palace. I wonder whether he called her "Jochebed" or "Mom." How would this scene have played out? Jochebed bringing her toddler to the palace to give him away *again*? And how would little Moses comprehend what was going on? Little boys don't care about money and huge houses. They want the embrace of their mama. My heart breaks for Moses and his mother. Did they have to rip Moses out of her hands and pull her out of the gates, kicking and screaming? Or was she calm and collected, knowing this was the best for her boy?

We will see whether this royal castle made all his dreams come true.

Essentially, the king's daughter adopted Moses, so he was now a prince. Moses's mom knew this was his best chance. I knew adoption would be my boy Nathan's best chance. Look what God says about adoption.

"But when the fullness of time had come, God sent forth his Son, born of woman, born under the law, to redeem those who were under the law, so that we might receive adoption as sons. And because you are sons, God has sent the Spirit of his Son into our hearts, crying, 'Abba! Father!' So you are no longer a slave, but a son, and if a son, then an heir through God. Formerly, when you did not know God, you were enslaved to those that by nature are not gods" (Galatians 4:4–8).

Not only did I give a child up for adoption, but *I* was adopted. You have been adopted. That is why Jesus came, to make you and me heirs to the throne. The King is now our Father, and we are to live in the royal castle with King Jesus.

The deepest and strongest foundation of adoption is located not in the act of humans adopting humans but in God adopting humans. And this act isn't part of His ordinary providence in the world; it is at the heart of the gospel. Galatians 4:4–5 is as central a gospel statement as there is: "But when the fullness of time had come, God sent forth his Son, born of woman, born under the law, to redeem those who were under the law, so that we might receive adoption as sons" (John Piper).

It wasn't until Jesus came that it was possible for us Gentiles (non-Jews) to be able to be part of the family. It is only because of Jesus's life, death, and resurrection that we can even have an opportunity to be saved through faith. If Jesus wouldn't have done the work on the cross, we would never have been able to be grafted into the family of God. He chose me. He chose you. He adopted me. He adopted you. "If you confess with your mouth that Jesus is Lord and believe in your heart that God raised him from the dead, you will be saved" (Romans 10:9).

Saved to live in his Stable Castle.

"For all who are led by the Spirit of God are sons of God. For you did not receive the spirit of slavery to fall back into fear, but you have received the Spirit of adoption as sons, by whom we cry, 'Abba! Father!' The Spirit himself bears witness with our spirit that we are children of God, and if children, then heirs—heirs of God and fellow heirs with Christ, provided we suffer with him in order that we may also be glorified with him" (Romans 8:14–17).

Nate and I never did stay in one house forever. In fact, thus far, we have lived in seven different houses. If I was still dependent on my old thinking that a house could make me secure or safe, then I would be miserable. With Jesus, I am now free to live anywhere and still be with Him, my Stable Castle.

CHAPTER 4

Deer in Headlights

I will give you a new heart and put a new spirit in you;
I will remove from you your heart of stone
and give you a heart of flesh.

—Ezekiel 36:26

By year seven of our marriage, we had three young children and were living in our second house. We were right up there with "the Joneses." On the outside we looked like a family to envy. We had the big, fancy house; the brand-new truck; and $3,000 watches. But we were in crazy amounts of debt. We lived paycheck to paycheck and had no business spending like we did. My husband had a five-year-old construction business, and we were starting to feel the squeeze of the recession. On top of all that, I quit my successful career as a stylist/salon owner. You are probably thinking, *Why on earth would you quit your job or buy a three-thousand-dollar watch?* Good questions.

A few months before, we had decided to "get some religion in the kids," so our first step was to have them dedicated to the Lord. By this time my mom had become a faithful Christ follower, and that was what her church did, dedicate the children. So we found a local church with similar beliefs and asked whether they would dedicate the kids. Now this was different from infant baptism, we learned, because we had already checked that box for ourselves, or our parents had. But a dedication was for the parents; they agreed to raise the kids in Christ. A baptism was for a believer to dedicate his or her life to Christ. Because our kids were too young to make that decision, we agreed to raise them to get to know Jesus. At the time we had *no* idea what that agreement meant. But we were sure we were doing it, because we were Americans, and we were good people and Christians, right?

That night I was presented with a question. "When you die and are standing at the pearly gates, what are you going to tell God the reason is for letting you into His heaven?"

I was like a deer in headlights. Time slowed down. I could vaguely hear my husband saying something about being a "good person," but I had nothing. I thought, *really? I'm not good enough to go to heaven? What is it I am doing with my life? Why do I still feel so alone when all my dreams have already come true? I have the guy, the kids, the career, the house. What is it I am missing? I've never hurt or killed anyone? How is it I am not good enough? And yet how could I be good enough?*

We prayed a salvation prayer that night with the pastor but really had no idea what was happening. We walked outside, and I expected the clouds to open up and angels to be singing, but nothing like that happened. Everything was normal, the same. That question sent me on a quest to find out the answer. What *will* I tell God? It caused me to ask a lot more questions.

The kids and I started attending church on Sunday mornings, and sometimes Nate came with us. The church started advertising an upcoming class. It was a twelve-week course on the basics of Christianity. The goal was to answer the basic questions. Why did Jesus have to die on the cross? Why read the Bible? Who is the Holy Spirit? Why and how to pray?

I decided I would bribe Nate into going to this class with me. I told him that if he went, I wouldn't complain about hunting season. Do I have any hunting widows out there? Holy moly.

Hunting brain is a totally new animal I never expected (that's another book). *Well*, Nate thought, *this won't last long, so sure.*

The fourth week was on why and how to pray. That theme really stuck with me. I had prayed in the past, sure. Whenever I needed God, I called on Him for a stoplight to turn green or for me not to be late for work and so forth. But prayer had never been a conversation with God. So that next morning I woke up early, about five thirty in the morning. I was going to meet my best friend. We had just finished a marathon the week before, and I was alone in the car. I decided to give this praying thing a try. That morning by myself I silently prayed to *the guy*, the God of the universe, Creator of all. That was the moment I was saved from my sins *and* forgiven. I felt a physical weight lifted off my shoulders. I had peace for the first time. Real joy for the first time. *None* of my circumstances changed, but my heart was new and soft, beating correctly for the first time. I didn't say any special words; in fact, I couldn't even tell you what I said. Somehow I knew my life had changed. I was free!

"I will give you a new heart and put a new spirit in you; I will remove from you your heart of stone and give you a heart of flesh" (Ezekiel 36:26). "An intimate encounter with Jesus is the most transforming experience of human existence. To know him is to come home. To have his life, joy, love, and presence cannot be compared. A true knowledge of Jesus is our greatest need and our greatest happiness. To be mistaken about him is the saddest mistake of all" [3]

Nothing on the outside looked any different, but I was forever changed on the inside. I tried to share this transformation with the people in my life, but only my mom and her husband seemed to understand what had happened to me. Nate said he felt different too, that he really liked going to church, and it made him feel better, but that was about it.

---

[3] John Eldredge, *Beautiful Outlaw*

Forty-seven days after my day in the car, we went to a family wedding. The first thing the Lord took from me was my desire for alcohol, so I was sober at this wedding. My husband was *not*. The morning after, he came to me and apologized for drinking too much, and he was sorry if he had embarrassed me. I replied with a simple, "You just drank too much." He went and lay on the couch, looking at his phone.

Then he came to me and said, "You have to listen to this song." One of his friends had posted a song on social media. I listened to it; I was very surprised *he* had listened to it. The song was very worshipful and sung by a woman. Now, my husband is a man's man. He is a construction worker, a heavy metal, hard rock kind of a guy. Not a woman-singing-worship-music kind of guy. The song was wonderful, but again, I was surprised.

We left the house to go pick up the kids. It just so happened that my mom had them for the night so we could go to the wedding. We were to pick them up at Mom's church the next morning. On the way there, I told Nate I was really emotional. I didn't know whether it was because of Christmastime or my period (you know the days, ladies) or this whole "God thing," but I was emotional. Then he said, "You are?" I looked over at my man's man, my big, tough, strong rock of a man, and he was *sobbing*. I was able to watch my husband go through the entire repentant process. He named off any and all of his sins, which he was convicted of, right there in the car beside me. He said Jesus had used that song to speak right to his heart. He was inconsolable.

We showed up my mom's church, and Nate cried through the whole service; and to be honest, for the next two days, he was changed, saved. Jesus was now his Savior and Lord of his life. Praise the Lord!

It was like our family was now walking in one direction, and this man, my man, grabbed ahold of his family and said, "No, we are *running* towards Jesus." He had never been more of a rock, never more respected by me and my kids, than at that moment when he led us to the Lord. Guys, if you ever think a man of God is weak, oh man, are you wrong! There is nothing stronger than a man who has Christ as his Lord. And ladies, if your husband isn't there yet, keep praying and seeking Jesus. Your family will follow.

I was blessed beyond belief to have my husband come with me on this journey only forty-eight days after I had surrendered. Clearly the Lord knew I wasn't strong enough on my own; he gave me a husband and brother in Christ so soon into my walk. Now that was the best thing that had happened to me thus far. Nate's conversion was so much better to watch than my own, but not everyone came along so easily.

Our transformation was so dramatic that I'm sure if I hadn't already been thought of as a stick of dynamite, I was now. Two weeks after I gave my life to Jesus, I quit my job and sold my stock in the salon. Somehow Nate agreed to this; he hadn't had his conversion yet. I must have been pretty convincing that this was a good idea because he truly was fine with it. I really couldn't understand why the Lord would have me leave the salon, because it really could have been a mission field. So many of my coworkers or friends at the salon thought so much like me. All of us were searching for significance, and I had found who mine was in. Christ could have used me to be a beacon of hope. I could have shared all that He had done for me and my family, but I kept sensing Him say that it spoke louder for me to leave than to stay. So I left.

Now we were living on only one income. I tried to do hair out of my house for a short while, but as soon as Nate met God, he was convicted that wasn't right. I needed to license my house to be able to do that. He said the Lord would provide. I remember thinking this kind of talk was so funny and foreign to us. When we said things like, "The Lord will provide" or "I don't know, let's pray about it," we would laugh at the sound of it on our tongues, but we still wholly believed it immediately. We both were completely sold out.

CHAPTER 5

Walk Like an Egyptian

All Scripture is inspired by God and profitable for teaching,
for reproof, for correction, for training in righteousness;
so that the man of God may be adequate,
thoroughly equipped for every good work.
—2 Timothy 3:16–17

In the book of Acts, the first deacon, Stephen, was giving an account of Moses's life, and then there was a turn. Stephen was explaining Moses's life of privilege in the palace and the exemplary education he had received. Moses had all the finest clothes, and I'm sure his watch cost way more than three thousand dollars. Then the story turned. Exodus 7:23 says that when Moses was forty years old, the desire came into his heart to visit his brothers, the children of Israel. Did he remember all this time that he was a Hebrew? Had he been brought up to know he was the adopted child? Or did it just hit him one day that the Hebrews were his people? Was his event like me in the car that day? Was it that Moses prayed and suddenly knew he was a child of the one true God? That his life had a purpose and calling? He must have had some idea of his call, because on his way to see his brothers (the Hebrew people), he saw one of them being wronged.

I'm sure Moses must have seen this mistreatment happening all the time. He was after all most likely an officer in the Egyptian army, so he would have been well acquainted with how the Hebrew people were being oppressed and beaten to do the work of the king. But this day was new; his eyes were opened, and he *had* to act. He looked this way and that, and then he struck down the Egyptian taskmaster and killed him. Verse 25 says he *supposed* his brothers would understand he was giving them salvation by his hand, but they didn't understand.

Have you ever had a good intention, even a great intention, but no one around you understood the great thing you were doing *for them*?

That was how a lot of the first months and even years went for my walk with the Lord. My eyes were opened, so I had to do something. I had to show everyone what he or she was doing wrong by living in bondage. *Be free! Live free like me.* I ran around, sharing what Christ had done in my life, but sometimes (especially more times than not in the beginning) I would say so in my own power, in my own timing, not willing to wait for His timing and direction. Let me tell you; it would blow up in my face. I *supposed* the people around me would understand I was just trying to save them. Maybe that was the problem; they didn't need *my* saving.

Like Moses, I had been trained for thirty-three years on how to be worldly. I had been literally trained on how to have worldly hair and dress like the world. I spoke like the world. Walked like the world. I did what the world did for thirty-three years, and then suddenly—bam!—I reached out to God, and I was free ... How did I *do* free?

I needed to be trained. I needed to be like 1 Timothy 3:16–17, which says I needed to be thoroughly equipped for every good work. *Thoroughly* equipped. Not just here and there equipped but all the way through, not doing anything halfway. I needed to be full-on equipped for *everything* God had for me, for every good work He had laid out for me. I need to be trained (and still do). So did Moses.

"The next day [after he killed the Egyptian], behold, two Hebrews were struggling together. And Moses said to the man in the wrong, 'Why do you strike your companion?' He answered, 'Who made you a prince and a judge over us? Do you mean to kill me as you killed the Egyptian?' Then Moses thought, 'Surely the thing is known.' When Pharaoh heard of it, he sought to kill Moses. But Moses fled from Pharaoh and stayed in the land of Midian" (Exodus 2:13–15).

Moses was busted. He thought that he had done the people of Israel a favor by killing one of the Egyptians, but that act backfired big time. He was now known as a murderer, not a savior. So Moses fled. He fled to the wilderness to get as far away from Pharaoh and his army as he could. He was scared and hiding. But God had other plans. *Hailey's Bible Handbook* explains Moses's trip to the wilderness this way: "This, in God's Providence, was part of Moses's training. The loneliness and roughness of the wilderness developed sturdy qualities hardly possible in the softness of the palace. It familiarized him with the region in which he was to lead Israel for 40 years."[4]

God saw Moses wasn't going to be able to fulfill the call on his life if he stayed in the comforts of the palace. God brought him out to train him. He loved Moses so much He was willing to take him out of his comfort zone and train him for his calling, destiny, and purpose. Not only that, but God also brought him to the exact place where he would later bring God's people. Moses unknowingly was scouting out the land he would later wander through. He learned how to be a shepherd. Moses was able to be fully trained and prepared for what lay before him. He didn't know what God was doing to prepare him, but God knew. As a shepherd, he would have known every square inch of the land.

Ray Vander Laan says *In the Dust of the Rabbi*, "God often

---

[4] Halley's Bible Handbook, Classic Edition: Completely Revised and Expanded; By: Henry H. Halley. 2014

chose shepherds to lead his people. Abram (Genesis 13:1–5), Moses (Exodus 3:1), and David (1 Samuel 17:14–15) for example, all were experienced shepherds. This image sent a powerful message to the people of Israel because even to this day a flock of sheep in Israel is dependent on the shepherd for survival. Israel is not a land of knee-high grass and abundant water. The shepherd must lead the sheep daily to graze on short tufts of grass on hillsides and to drink from widely scattered sources of water. Without the shepherd's leading, the flock would die."[5]

Moses needed to be trained to be a *good* shepherd. He was being trained *by* the Good Shepherd. God was showing him where all the short tufts of grass were and where to go for a drink. God was leading Moses and showing him how to be a leader of his people for forty more years *so* he could be ready, prepared to fulfill his calling to be a good shepherd to the Israelites (whether they knew it or not).

This makes me think. What has God taken me out of *so* I would be trained, prepared, and ready for His calling on my life? I see now that I needed a trip out into the wilderness to see how to be a child of God.

Our friends started distancing themselves from us. The gap of our interests started to become painfully evident. I was no longer interested in the things I used to be interested in. I didn't want to complain about my husband or make fun of other people. I didn't want to plan drunken weekends. Things changed, and *I'm* the one who disrupted the apple cart. I was the one who changed the

---

[5] In the Dust of the Rabbi by Ray Vander Laan (2006, Paperback)

playing field of the friendships around me. So people started to distance themselves from me and my family.

This was especially hard on me. I am extremely extroverted, so not having friends to share this new life with was excruciating. Losing my best friend was especially painful. She would say things like, "All you ever want when we talk is for me to be saved." Although yes, this was true, I didn't realize how it felt to her. To her, I wasn't listening to anything she had going on; I just wanted her to know Jesus. She grew up a lot like I did and was taught that if you are a "good person," then you're fine; heaven is in your future. She didn't need all this Jesus talk. Her faith was private, and I was all in her private business. I, on the other hand, would get excited about a new mascara and want *everyone* to know about it, so when I found the Savior of the world, you can imagine how much I thought *everyone* needed to know this, especially the people I loved. Needless to say, we both were left with broken hearts.

I told Nate, "Well, I guess you're *it* now. *You're* my friend. You will get *all* my words each day."

This declaration, of course, terrified him, and he said, "No way! You need some friends."

In my desperation for a Christian friend, I called a woman from the class we had taken and just said plainly, "I need a friend. Will you be my friend?" Thankfully she said yes, and I was so grateful to the Lord that she didn't go running for the hills.

Erwin McManus puts it this way in his book Last Arrow. "If you want to get somewhere fast, go at it alone. If you want to go far, go together and if you want to go far fast, GoTRIBE."

I needed a new tribe, one that would be walking alongside me. Not one on a pedestal but one that was next to me, cheering me on. To follow Christ so close, we get the dust of His sandals on our faces. We will trip and fall and make mistakes, but our number one goal is grace and obedience to the Father.

C. S. Lewis wrote, "In each of my friends there is something that only some other friend can fully bring out. By myself I am not large enough to call the whole man into activity; I want other lights than my own to show all his facets ... Hence true Friendship is the least jealous of loves. Two friends delight to be joined by a third, and three by a fourth, if only the newcomer is qualified to become a real friend. They can then say, as the blessed souls say in Dante, 'Here comes one who will augment our loves.' For in this love 'to divide is not to take away.'"

I couldn't just depend on my one new friend. I needed more true friendships in my life to bring out *all* of me—to live out what God has for me but also to show me all the parts of God. My friend Milissa's reaction to God was completely different from my friend Amber's reaction. This gives me more of a picture of who God is through the eyes of my different friends. I wouldn't know God as well as I do without these ladies.

In his book *The Four Loves*, C. S. Lewis said that when one of his friends died, he had to grieve *that* as well as grieving the way that friend had showed him Christ or how that friend had brought out a certain laughter in another friend. It was lost and gone too with the death. We need community.

Think of the example God gives to us. Even in Himself He has community through the Father, the Son, and the Holy Spirit. They all work together perfectly, complementing one another and bringing out the best in one another. Even God wants community. Isolation is so dangerous.

It seems to me that life is like a swinging pendulum. I swing to the right and then to the left, right, left, right—never really landing in the middle, never pausing in mid swing. I'm constantly swinging from the far right to the far left. I have many friends and then swing all the way to no friends. I went from not knowing God at all to being more intimate with Him than I ever have with anyone, swinging on a diet with five hundred calories (literally have done that one) to eating four thousand calories a day. The pendulum never seems to stop.

Moses went from a palace full of servants, chefs, and royalty. He was used to looking out his stone window ledge to a vast mountainside full of slaves, surrounding him at all hours of the day, and loud gongs of construction all around. His army was constantly preparing for war, sparring with one another, swords scraping and shields banging. He heard the clanging of pots and pans during the preparing of his every meal, right on time each day. His servants scurried down the halls to make this thriving metropolis run each and every day like a well-oiled machine. Moses was right in the middle of all of it. Then he swung all the way to the other side, never pausing in the middle, never saying, "I think I'm going to just live in the suburbs for a while, find out what suburbia is like." Nope. He swung all the way to the wilderness.

After Moses took matters into his own hands and killed the Egyptian taskmaster, the word says, "When Pharaoh heard of it, he sought to kill Moses. But Moses fled from Pharaoh and stayed in the land of Midian. And he sat down by a well" (Exodus 2:15).

Finally, he found a well far in the desert. He sat down beside it. He was hungry and thirsty, and his ears rang from the silence. *What just happened?* he thought. *How did I end up here alone? I thought I was doing well. How did they not know I was helping them? Why couldn't they see I was for them?*

I'm not sure who I am speaking for here, Moses or myself.

But he sat and waited, too tired to draw his own water. "Seven daughters came and drew water and filled their troughs to water their father's flock" (Exodus 2:16).

I imagine Moses looked at this and thought, *What? Where did they come from?* While the women were working, shepherds came down from the field and tried to push the women out from using the well. Moses found his strength, his purpose; he would help these women.

"When the daughters went home their father was amazed they were able to get their work done and be back so soon. So they told their dad, 'An Egyptian delivered us out of the hand of the shepherds and even drew water for us and watered the flock'" (Exodus 2:19).

The Egyptian delivered us? The Egyptian? Moses wasn't Egyptian; he was a Hebrew. Why would they think he was Egyptian?

When I first accepted Christ and started doing a Bible study, I quickly became friends with the leader of our women's ministry. I remember thinking, *Her life must be so much easier than mine because everyone knows she works for the church. She is all "churchy." No one questions her music choices or what she does with her weekends. No one is asking her to bend her morals or toe the line. They all just know she is a Christian, and they expect her to act like one.* I remember thinking life would be so much easier if everyone knew I had a new job with the church, that I was a Christian now, not some heathen pretending I was better than everyone else. I'm not "using *Jesus* as a scapegoat for all my problems," they would say, thick with sarcasm; or at least that was what it *felt like* they (the people in my pre-Christ life) were saying.

Maybe Moses felt the same way. If only he had grown up with his Hebrew people, these women wouldn't have thought he was an Egyptian, but that wasn't the case. Moses spoke like an Egyptian. I spoke like the world spoke. He dressed like an Egyptian. I dressed like the world dressed. His prep school education was from the Egyptians. I was a public school kid (might be a slight difference there); I was schooled in the world.

He walked like an Egyptian. (You have to sing the song, Walk like an Egyptian, when you say that.)

I walked like the world. I needed to go out into the wilderness, and feel and hear the silence. I needed to sit down and wait for my calling, destiny, and purpose in life. I needed the wilderness to see my purpose.

Disclaimer: I *love*, love, love all my people from my past. I am friends with a lot of them again. But this journey was mine to walk alone; I needed to be shoved (hard) into taking those painful first steps.

Some of the first questions I asked were these: Could I be trained in the wilderness not to desire approval by dressing provocatively? Could I believe I was (am) worth so much more than that? Was I worth more than being the "loud talker" at the bar? Was I worth more than the pounding headache in the morning or, worse, the walk of shame from yet another mistake with the same disrespectful guy over and over again?

Jesus had a wilderness of His own. Just like mine, His started right when He went public with His faith.

Jesus had a cousin named John. John's entire mission in life was to make way for the Messiah. He lived in the great outdoors. He preached and baptized anyone who came to him. He preached, "Repent and make way for the Lord" over and over. People were baptized because of his message of Christ.

> As it is written in the book of the words of Isaiah
> the prophet,
> The voice of one crying in the
> wilderness:
> "Prepare the way of the Lord,
> Every Valley shall be filled,
> and every mountain and hill shall
> be made low,
> and the crooked shall become
> straight,
> and the rough places shall
> become level ways,
> and all flesh shall see the salvation
> Of God." (Luke 3:4–6)

This is what he would say to the crowds when they came out to be baptized by him. He would yell at them for all the terrible things they were doing, and they would say, "What then shall we do?" (Luke 3:10). John basically told them to love God and love people. It's as simple as that. So they asked him whether he was the Christ, the Messiah they had been waiting for. Up until this point, the Jewish people (same as a Hebrew or an Israelite) were still waiting for a savior. They didn't know the baby's cry on Christmas night had been their awaited Messiah. So they asked John whether he was the one.

"John answered them all, saying, 'I baptize with water, but he who is mightier than I is coming, the strap of whose sandals I am not worthy to untie. He will baptize with the Holy Spirit and fire'" (Luke 3:16). This was John's purpose, to be "John the Baptist." To make the way for Jesus, this was what he had been born to do—to educate the people, lead them to Jesus, and, when they believe, baptize them. So when Jesus walked up to the river, John continued to point to Jesus and say, "There *He* is!"

Jesus even came to the water to be baptized by John. "And when Jesus was baptized, immediately he went up from the water, and behold, the heavens were opened to him, and he saw the Spirit of God descending like a dove and coming to rest on him; and behold, a voice from heaven said, 'This is my beloved Son, with whom I am well pleased'" (Matthew 3:16–17).

Immediately after Jesus's baptism, "Jesus was led by the Spirit into the wilderness to be tempted by the devil" (Matt 4:1). The Spirit of God led Jesus into the wilderness. He was bringing Him into His training ground. Jesus, being fully man and fully God, still walked in the wilderness for forty days and forty nights without food. The enemy tempted him over and over. The enemy even used the scriptures to tempt Jesus, but Jesus *knew* the word of God—*He is the Word*. The scriptures can sadly be used for evil when abused or used out of context. But if we know the Word, who Jesus is, then we are armed for the wilderness. God used the wilderness to train Jesus and to train me.

"In the beginning was the Word, and the Word was with God, and the Word was God. He was in the beginning with God. All things were created through him, and without him was not anything made that was made. In him was life, and the life was the light of men. The light shines in the darkness, and the darkness has not overcome it" (John 1:1–5).

The questions I had about my worth were all answered during my wilderness walk, and they were answered by the Word, Jesus Himself. I am worth more than how I dress or speak. I am worth waiting for and listening to, because Christ came and walked this earth just like I am doing and was tempted just as I get tempted. He is the victory I can stand on.

After I was brought into the wilderness of no friends, home, or toys, then and only then would I be ready for my tribe God had waiting for me.[6] I would be ready for my seven women to walk up to my well and draw water for me *so* I would be able to draw water for *them*, so I would be able to speak life into them. I would someday release my insecurities and self-doubt so I could fill up with Jesus, so He could overflow to the people around me, so the world wouldn't pour out of me, but life would pour out of me. "You prepare a table before me in the presence of my enemies; You have anointed my head with oil; My cup overflows" (Psalm 23:5).

The wilderness is the only place to meet God and be totally broken. The wilderness is where you get ready for Him to pick up each piece and glue each back together in its perfect place. Not so the pieces fit tightly together but so there are holes and creases; then when I would be so filled with His light, it would

---

[6] 2008 recession hit us hard, we lost our home, cars and toys all that year. Major humble pie.

burst through all my cracks and creases. It would burst through all the spaces of my imperfect life so He would be the only one seen.

This happens in the wilderness.

Let me tell you more about my imperfect life. Let me tell you about one of my gaping holes.

CHAPTER 6

Plague of Shame

Fixing our eyes on Jesus, the author and perfecter of faith,
who for the joy set before him endured the cross,
despising the shame, and has sat down
at the right hand of the throne of God.

—Hebrews 12:2

A few years into my walk with Jesus, I still had this haunting plague in my life. I thought it was a weight issue. If only I could be skinny, then I wouldn't be plagued by this sadness.

Unfortunately, when you accept Christ, you bring your humanness into your relationship. Some things can be miraculously taken away, like my desire for comfort in drinking alcohol. That was gone immediately, but *this* was lingering. I had spent a lifetime learning and training myself that being overweight made me lesser or undesirable as a person. I even had a friend who had a dream that I was super skinny with blonde hair and big boobs. But I was a terrible person, and she didn't like me. I was actually surprised by this. If I was really honest with myself, I even thought my friends would like me better if I was thinner, like somehow that affected who I was and what they thought of me.

Now that I had the love of God, I *knew* I shouldn't care about my physical appearance so much. Be healthy, yes, but do not dwell on being magazine ready. So this knowledge that my thinking was unhealthy sent me into countless hours of prayer and talking the issue out with girlfriends. What is it? Vanity? Food addiction? Gluttony? What is my sin in this? I wanted to know so badly so I could repent and turn from it, but nothing seemed to work. I read this:

> I know I am not alone in the nagging sense of failing to measure up, a feeling of not being good enough as a woman. Every woman I've ever met feels it—something deeper than just the sense of failing at what she does. An underlying, gut feeling of failing at who she is. I am not enough and I am too much all at the same time. Not pretty enough, not thin enough, not kind enough, not gracious enough, not disciplined enough. But too emotional, too needy, too sensitive, too strong, too opinionated, too messy. The result is Shame, the universal companion of women. It haunts us, nipping at our heels, feeding on our deepest fear that we will end up abandoned and alone.[7]

These words jumped off the page and into my heart. Ooooh, shame. Yes, that makes sense. I am not alone in this. Here's a sigh of relief, but the shame I brought on myself, right? Deserved shame?

The year I was pregnant, my mom and I were frantic to find a dress for me to wear to Easter church. Remember, this was one of the holidays I *knew* I had to attend church, because that's what *good* people do. So here is the scene. I was sixteen years old in the 1990s before cute maternity clothes were a thing (I never owned one piece of maternity clothing), so I finally found

---

[7] Captivating: Unveiling The Mystery Of A Woman's Soul, By: John and Staci Eldridge, 2005

this outfit at a complete mom store like Christopher & Banks or somewhere like that. It was a pair of stretchy *printed* pants and a baggy blouselike top. Cringe. It was an outfit that *screamed*, "Your mom dressed you!"

We are walking through her huge church, and she gave me a side hug, trying to comfort me, and said, "Oh, honey, I'm so sorry. Everyone sins, but yours is just obvious to everyone."

I truly think she was trying to comfort me, but she was in her beginning walk at the time. She was in her "Do things in your own strength 75 percent of the time" phase. Not to mention she too was human, but it still hurt. I deserved the shame, I told myself. It was my choice, and I had made it. "He does not treat us as our sins deserve or repay us according to our iniquities" (Psalm 103:10). Thank God!

Guilt says you *did* something wrong, and shame says you *are* something wrong.

Thankfully Jesus died for our guilt *and* shame. He paid the price for our sins and the guilt of our sins: past, present, and future. How can this be possible? This is way too simple, right?

Let's go back to where I started this chapter. I was so crippled by this question I had. What was my sin in this weight thing?

I was given the opportunity to have two women sit down with me and do some intentional, strategic, guided prayer. The lead woman's name was Pam. I knew this was going to be a three-hour commitment. Better an hour of prayer than a year of counseling, right? Well, that was how I went into it. I was going to do this or start meeting with someone who specialized in eating disorders. The problem I had with the words "eating disorder" was that I wasn't starving myself, and I wasn't binge eating and purging either, not really. I knew whatever I was doing wasn't working because I still had this haunting feeling that would leave me restless and depressed. *What is the deal? I should be free. After all, I am a child of God.* I was now a Christian, but I was still haunted by … something.

I knew this thinking was vain and superficial, but still here I was, spinning my wheels to get it together. I was desperate to get help. Before I showed up for this prayer meeting on a crisp October day, I had filled out a ten-page questionnaire. That was fun. So when I showed up, these women already had an idea of what was happening with me.

At first they thought I had a performance issue, but after speaking with me and hearing me use the word *haunted*, they realized my problem was much deeper than a performance issue. We all prayed, and Pam (the woman leading me in prayer) asked whether shame and abandonment resonated with me. Of course, shame was a no-brainer. I knew I *should* feel shame (remember, not all beliefs are correct). After all, teen pregnancy, hello? But the abandonment really took me by surprise. Then she started using other words that were attached to abandonment like *unwanted, unneeded, left behind, undeserving*, all those words I heard in my mind every day.

We spent some time praying against shame and abandonment.

This reminds me of this verse in Jeremiah; "I will cleanse them from all their iniquity by which they have sinned against me, and I will pardon all their iniquities by which they have sinned against me and by which they have transgressed against me" (Jeremiah 33:8).

Oh, Jeremiah, I just love you! You pleaded with your people to repent and turn away from their sins. They never did listen. Could you imagine a completely unsuccessful ministry? Jeremiah was giving the Jewish people hope for their Messiah, our Jesus. Jeremiah was essentially saying, "Turn from your sin, and He will take it from you. He will nail it to the cross with Himself. He who is without sin will become sin for you! All you have to do is turn. Why are you not listening?" Jeremiah would shout.

That day I heard the truth, I heard loud and clear who I was, who I am *in* Christ!

Because of what Jesus did on the cross and because the Father raised Him from the dead. Did you hear that? Raising Him from the dead? Jesus *died*! He was dead for three days. He had all the weight of our sin—of my sin, of your sin—on Him. He took it to hell for us so we wouldn't have to live there for eternity.

Argh. I have a lump in my throat, tears welling up. Thank You, Savior! He took all the shame to hell and left it there. Never to return with Him.

Then.

Then.

Then!

The Father raised Him to life, clean, new, restored, white as snow, free from all sin.

"Christ was raised from the dead by the glory of the Father, we too might walk in newness of life" (Romans 6:4).

I chose life. What do you choose?

Remember Moses? He went through his training in the wilderness. He learned how to be a follower of God, of the one true God, but he had all his people, left in Egypt, worshipping false gods. They worshipped animal gods. *Hailey's Bible Handbook* says, "In various temples the sacred animals were fed, groomed and cared for in the most luxurious way, by great colleges of priests. Of all the animals, the Bull was the most sacred. Incense and sacrifices were offered before the Sacred Bull. The animal on its death was embalmed, and with pomp and ceremony fitting for a king. Buried like a king. The crocodile also was greatly honored: waited on, in his temple at Tains, by 50 or more priests. This was the religion that was nurtured around the Hebrew people for 400 years."[8]

---

[8] Halley's Bible Handbook, Classic Edition: Completely Revised and Expanded; By: Henry H. Halley. 2014

This was what Moses grew up doing and seeing and being educated on. He was made to think this was worship, that this was normal. He was taught that a bull was more sacred than a person, that a frog or gnat deserved his praise, or that waiting on a crocodile was of high regard. Something to strive toward, something to brag about to your friends. Something for your mom to brag to her friends about. "Oh, yeah? Well, my son serves the crocodile god. What does your son do?" This sounds crazy to us. Why would they believe this, right? I would *never*, right? Or would I?

So Moses's trip to the wilderness is so much more understandable now. We can see that he needed some major deprogramming, and he got it. Now Moses was eighty years old, and God remembered His people left in slavery, surrounded by false gods and animal worship. God's people had been surrounded by all this for four hundred years. How many generations is that? Four, five, six? By this time, no one knew anyone who had seen God's greatness. All they knew were slavery and the stories of Adam and Eve, Noah, Abraham, Jacob, Isaac, Joseph, and so forth. These were the stories passed down from generation to generation. They didn't have a book, manual, or Bible to show them who their God is or was. But they were still filled with the faith and knowledge of the God of Jacob, Abraham, and Isaac. The God of them! But why wasn't He setting them free? Why was this bad, terrible, horrible thing continuing to happen to them? They were stuck in slavery with no out.

"The Lord said to Moses, 'When you go back to Egypt, see that you do before Pharaoh all the miracles that I have put in your power. But I will harden his heart, so that he will not let the people go'" (Exodus 4:21).

God was saying to Moses. "Okay, it is time. Go back and show the king how powerful I am. God is going to make it so he won't be able to see it for a while, because *He wants it that way.* He wants it to be known to *everyone* that He is God! So this is going to take some time."

So the signs, plagues, and wonders happened, otherwise known as plagues. Over and over again, God plagued the Egyptian people with plagues, which directly went against the "gods" they had been serving. They worshipped frogs. *Oh, let's put frogs everywhere, I mean everywhere. In the oven, in your bed, on your person, eve-ry-where!*

So the people of Egypt are infested with frogs. I mean, picture this for a moment. Everywhere. In your bed? I mean, come on! And they worshipped frogs, so it wasn't like they could kill them or throw them out. So they lived with the frogs in the bed, in the oven, in their bowls, at work, at school, at Starbucks, everywhere. Then Moses asked Pharaoh, "When would you like me to get rid of the frogs for you? Ummm … now! Right?"

"Nope," Pharaoh said. "Tomorrow."

"What? Tomorrow? Are you kidding me? Why tomorrow? Why not yesterday? I would have said yesterday for sure! I think, right?"

This makes me think to myself, do I have some frogs in *my* bed. Is there a false god, "a frog" I have placed my trust in? Do I have some fears looming in the darkness that I haven't quite trusted God with just yet? Or maybe my faith is so little that I think God will need some time to get "that thing" done. Maybe a day will help him to fulfill that. Maybe I'm not quite ready to give up my frogs. Maybe I think I deserve the frogs. They are a reminder of the terrible things I've done, and I deserve to have them hang out for a while. Maybe tomorrow I will be ready to be free. Maybe tomorrow.

Tomorrow is a lie. What we have available is now. We have a God who has given us this amazing book of examples of what to do and what not to do, but more than that, it shows us who He is, how He is love, and who He says we are *now*. This isn't an ancient god who isn't relevant today! I almost wish I couldn't relate to the frogs, but I can. I am human, and I need the truth of God's word to remind me over and over *who I am*.

Here are a few truths about who you are if you have given your life over to Christ Jesus, confessed with your mouth, and believe He died on the cross for your sins and defeated death on the third day. Then this is your truth as well.

- 1 Corinthians 6:17 says, "I am united with the Lord and one with him in spirit."
- 1 Corinthians 6:20 says, "I have been bought with a price—I belong to God."
- Ephesians 1:1 says, "I am a saint."
- Colossians 2:10 says, "I am complete in Christ."
- Romans 8:1–2 says, "I am free from condemnation."
- Romans 8:31–34 says, "I am free from any condemning charges against me."
- John 15:16 says, "I have been chosen and appointed to bear fruit."

If you are still at the place where you don't know whether you believe this whole Savior thing, stay with me. Maybe you are riddled with questions like these: Where is God when I was hurt? Where was He when my family was hurt or died? Where is He now in *this* struggle I'm going through? I am hoping to show you where He is and has always been.

Not tomorrow but *now* and forever.

CHAPTER 7

The Burning Bush

I will hear what God the Lord will say;
For He will speak peace to His people, to His godly ones;
But let them not turn back to folly.

—Psalm 85:8

We are going to back up a little in our story to the place where Moses was shepherding, not people-herding yet. Day after day Moses was out tending to his flock and doing the mundane work of his day—laundry, meals, cleaning, laundry, meals, cleaning, laundry. Oh, I mean sheep, sheep, sheep.

This week I learned that at night the shepherds from all the nearby areas would get together at night and gather all of their flocks to one place. This place would have a stone fence all the way around it, with only one way to enter the fold (sheep talk for a group of sheep).

Say that ten shepherds come with each of their one hundred sheep. Nine of the shepherds would go home to sleep at night, and one shepherd would stay. He was called the porter.

The porter's job was to protect that gate. It was the only way a predator could get in. He would lie down at the opening and sleep there, so if anything tried to come after the fold, they would have to go through him.

Then in the morning the shepherds woke up early, kissed their wives, and headed back out to their flocks. When each shepherd got to the gate, he would have to be identified by the porter as safe, and then he could enter the fold and *call* his flock. This was a strange concept to me at first. There were one thousand sheep. Sheep = dumb animals. If you know much about sheep, you know they aren't known for their smarts. But they know their shepherd's voice. When their shepherds call them, they run to follow.

I have seen this at the nursery of a church or day care. All the children are playing loudly, totally engrossed in what they are doing with their friends, but the moment they hear their mom's or dad's voice, only *their* child looks up. No one else even hears it. They don't know their voice; that voice isn't *their* daddy's.

So one by one the shepherds call their flocks out of the fold and back under the protection of their good shepherd. Moses had learned to be a good shepherd. "Now Moses was keeping the flock of his father-in-law, Jethro, the priest of Midian, and he led his flock to the West side of the wilderness and came to Horeb, the mountain of God. And an angel of the Lord appeared to him in a flame of fire out of the midst of a bush. He looked, and behold, the bush was burning, yet it was not consumed. And Moses thought 'I will turn aside to see this great sight, why the bush is not burned'" (Exodus 3:1–3)

This cracks me up to think about Moses walking along, minding his own business; and suddenly he saw something out of the corner of his eye. Then he thought, *Huh, what is that? I think I should go check that out. I am going to turn and go this direction so I can see more clearly.*

Then look at what happened next in verse 4. "When the Lord saw that he had turned aside to see, God called to him out of the bush, 'Moses, Moses!' And he said, 'Here I am.'"

How many times have I walked right past the burning bushes in my life? Scripture says that God didn't say anything to Moses until he turned. *When* God saw that Moses had turned to see Him, *then* He called him.

When I turned and said, "Lord, I can't do this on my own," *then* He called me to Himself. When I turned from the distractions of life to talk to Him, *then* He spoke clearly to me. And just like the sheep, I heard His voice clearly because I knew Him intimately. I followed His voice even when I didn't know where we were going. But I knew He was good. "Jesus said, 'Truly, truly, I say to you, I am the door of the sheep. All who came before me are thieves and robbers, but the sheep did not hear them. I am the door; if anyone enters through me, he will be saved, and will go in and out and find pasture. The thief comes only to steal and kill and destroy; I came that they may have life, and have it abundantly. I am the good shepherd; the good shepherd lays down his life for the sheep'" (John 10:7–11).

Jesus *is* the door. He *is* the place where the porter would lay down to protect his sheep. He is the Good Shepherd. He laid down His life for His followers. Christ is the burning bush in the wilderness, calling your name.

What is distracting you from seeing the burning bush in your life? God is right there, ready to speak if you would just *turn* to Him. Take a few minutes, put this book down, and spend time with God, confessing the distractions you have put in front of hearing from Him. After you have had your time with Him, come back because I want you to do something else with Him before you're done.

This is the place where I was left in the prayer meeting. I had repented for believing the lies of shame and abandonment. I was free of them, but I needed to hear from God on what to replace them with. I didn't want to be all willy-nilly and pretend I could stay free and not pick these things back up, so I needed to be trained to hear God's voice clearly and be able to articulate it in a safe space.

Now I have gotten rid of shame and abandonment in my mind. What next? Let's fill back up with truth. First, I want to show you one way to hear the voice of God. We can do it together. This isn't anything weird. Just humor me for a minute.

1. Count to ten *aloud.*
2. Now count to ten again but this time count only one to five aloud. Then count six to ten in your head.

Okay, so what did the voice sound like in your head? Someone else's voice? A man's voice? Or was it *your* voice?

That is the still, small voice God uses! *But* hear me; the same voice can speak lies to you in your head. So how do we know who is speaking to us or what is truth and what is a lie? Well, I'm so glad you asked.

Let's start with the enemy. What do we know about him?

> You are of your father the devil, and you want to do the desires of your father. He was a murderer from the beginning, and *does not stand in the truth* because there is *no truth in him.* Whenever he speaks a *lie,* he speaks from his own nature, for he is a *liar and the father of lies.* (John 8:44 emphasis added)

> Be of sober spirit, be on the alert. Your adversary, the devil prowls around like a roaring lion, *seeking someone to devour.* (1 Peter 5:8 emphasis added)

> The one who *practices sin* is of the devil; for the devil has sinned from the beginning. The Son of God appeared for this purpose, to destroy the works of the devil. (1 John 3:8 emphasis added)

> And the *tempter* came and said to Him [Jesus],
> "If You are the Son of God, command that these
> stones become bread." (Matthew 4:3 emphasis
> added)

The Enemy, the Devil

Who is he?

- He is a murderer.
- He doesn't stand on truth.
- There is no truth in him.
- He is a liar.
- He seeks people to devour.
- He practices sin.
- He is a tempter.

He can do all these things if he wants, but lying to us, seeking to destroy us, tempting us to practice sin—these aren't a sin for us. If we are oppressed but do not lash out at our neighbor because of it, then the oppression isn't sin. That is just a tactic of the enemy to try to get us to sin. If he tempts me with gossip but I don't share with my friend the latest juicy gossip, then being tempted to gossip isn't the sin. Only acting on the temptation would be a sin.

He also can't read our minds or know the future. The Bible tells us that only God is omniscient, not angels or fallen angels. "As for you, my son Solomon, know the God of your father, and serve him with a whole heart and a willing mind; for the Lord searches all hearts, and understands every intent of the thoughts. If you seek him, he will let you find him" (1 Chronicles 28:9).

Only God knows every intent of our thoughts. That fact can be daunting to me sometimes. He knows *all* my thoughts? *All* of them? There are some thoughts I would like to keep to myself.

There are many actions I would rather keep to myself, let alone my thought life.

Wow. This was a really heavy thing for me to carry when I first met Christ. Seriously, I'm never alone? Like never? This can give almost a claustrophobic feeling, with no escape, no place to run or hide. But then I got to know the One who was always with me. He—the One who will never leave me or forsake me, the life-giving One, the Provider, the Immanuel, God with us, the One who heals, the Peacemaker, my Companion, The One who *sees* me! That Guy—I don't ever *want* that Guy to leave.

Since the enemy is a liar, deceiver, tempter, one who is *not* all knowing, he wouldn't know the future. So he would talk to us only about our past. He lies to us about our past, tempts us to practice sin, and tempt us not to stand on truth. But once we have eyes to see his schemes, we then can arm ourselves for battle. Oh, how many times I have fallen for his schemes. What do we do to combat this? "Submit therefore to God. Resist the devil and he will flee from you" (James 4:7).

Think of him as a cockroach. You are sitting in your home, minding your own business, when suddenly—bam! You realize you have a nasty, gross, huge cockroach in your house. Yuck! You run around in the dark, squatting and swinging at it, but to no avail. This cockroach just keeps dodging and tormenting you. You finally give up for the night and go to bed, but you cannot sleep. How could you? This thing could crawl into your bed at any moment. You shut your eyes to try to get some Zs, but then you hear a scratching.

What was that? Your heart is racing. Deep breaths. Okay, it was nothing. You calm yourself back down, and again you hear something. *Argh, this is so frustrating!* Finally, you get up and turn on the light. He flees. He crawls back into whatever hole he came from. He's gone, and you can sleep. All you needed to do is turn on the light, and he will flee. James is saying the very same thing. Turn on the light of truth in the scriptures, and the devil must flee. Stop running around in the dark. Stop swatting and swinging without your eyes opened. "The word is a lamp to my feet and a light to my path" (Psalm 119:105). The living word of God not only lights the way but also shows you what is in your way.

Now that we know, the cockroach Satan is a liar and deceiver, and he lies only about the past and tempts us to practice sin in the future. Now let's look at what the Holy Spirit would talk to us about. First, *not* the past. Jesus died for our sins—past, present, and future. He won't remember them as far as the East is from the West. If we keep confessing the same sin (in other words, sex before marriage), He's like, "What? You had sex before you got married? No, you didn't. That was forgiven! You are clean, white as snow. I took on that shame and guilt on the cross. I brought that sin down to the depths of hell and left it there *so you* could be free! Be free!"

Jesus's message is full of truth, hope, love, and peace. He is truth. He is love. He is the God of peace. "The fruit of the Spirit is love, joy, peace, patience, kindness, goodness, faithfulness, and self-control" (Eph. 5:22).

These are the things God will be talking to you about: hope for the future, conviction in missing the mark, forgiveness, peace, joy, kindness, encouragement to do good, not to grow weary. But most of all, He speaks to us about love.

"Love is patient, love is kind; love does not envy or boast; it is not arrogant or rude. It does not insist on its own way; it is not irritable to resentful; it does not rejoice at wrongdoing, but rejoices with the truth. Love bears all things, believes all things, hopes all things, endures all things. Love never ends" (1 Corinthians 4–8).

For many years I believed that if I would have gone into my marriage as a virgin, everything would have been better. I looked at couples who got married while pure and free from sexual sin and thought, *Wow, they are so lucky to be starting perfectly.* I couldn't see how they could ever have any problems. Many of the issues in my marriage seemed to revolve around sex. I would compare our sex life (meaning how often we had sex) to the people around me. I assumed everyone else had sex all the time. Women would always, it seemed to me, talk about how they couldn't get dressed in front of their husbands because he would "get the wrong idea." This never happened in my house. I could walk around naked and felt like my husband didn't even take a second look. I took this as a sign; I was obviously disgusting and not worth chasing after.

So my self-worth plummeted every time the subject came up. I thought that maybe if I had never had sex before we got married, then it would still be fresh and exciting for us to explore one another. Or if I just worked out, ate better, and was skinny, then my husband would jump me in the middle of the day. This was an area I didn't think God was interested in fixing, because let's face it; it's sex, and God doesn't care about that. That's dirty and not an issue to bring to God. Plus, I had done this to myself. I chose to have sex before I got married, and now I am going to have to live with the consequences.

It turns out that God cares a lot about sex; actually He invented it. I didn't find this out until I had to give our oldest daughter "the talk." I was telling her about how God had created this beautiful, amazing thing for a husband and a wife to share. I told her sex was beautiful, special, and an exciting thing God uses to make a man and woman one. It was something to look forward to but not to take lightly.

After our talk, I thought, *Was that for her or for me?* Sex isn't dirty and shameful like I had been brought up to believe. Our culture twists and turns it into something to be done in the dark and in secret without boundaries. Yes, of course, sex is a special, private thing between a man and a woman, but when it is how God intended between a husband and wife, it is to be celebrated and made a priority.

I heard someone say once that a marriage without sex is like a song without music. A poem is nice and can be beautiful, but when you put it to music ... magic!

This new understanding of sex caused me to feel as if I could bring my sin of sex before marriage to God and receive His forgiveness. God wants me free of this sin and free to enjoy my marriage for all He has in it. Until I saw that God even cared about sex, I didn't think He would be able to redeem my sin.

Both my husband and I had some work we needed to do with God. We had to go *separately* to the feet of Jesus, confess our sins, and receive His forgiveness. We couldn't fix ourselves or our marriage by comparing our marriage to other marriages. We needed to sit face-to-face with our Creator, our audience of One.

After listening to my story, is there anything that comes up in you for which you need to confess and asked forgiveness? We as humans need to confess and even say our sin aloud to release ourselves from the power of sin. We need forgiveness from God so we can move on from sin. If there is anything, confess it now and accept the amazing forgiveness that Jesus died for and move on. If you're holding on to the lie that your sin is too much for Jesus to forgive or Him dying on the cross wasn't enough for that sin, don't do that!

How could we believe that? How could I say my sin is bigger than what You did, Jesus? What more could You or I do that is bigger than the God of this universe sending His only begotten Son to earth as a baby and thirty-three years later dying an excruciating death on a cross? Then take all our sins on that cross and drag them all down to the pit of hell. If He would have stayed dead, stayed in hell, that wouldn't have been that remarkable. Ten out of ten people die. So He would have been like everyone else. He died like everyone else. But the story doesn't end there! He didn't just die. He rose from the grave. He defeated death. He defeated sin. He defeated guilt. He defeated shame. He defeated. Period. So that …

We wouldn't have to. We *get* to live in that victory. We are on the victory side. My pastor signs every e-mail that way. "On the victory side, Pastor Dave." What an amazing reminder. We are on the victory side. We are not fighting *for* victory; we fight *from* victory!

Let's do battle from the victory side.

When our hearts are open to detect God's fingerprints of providence, when our hearts are reminded of His never-ending care for us, our internal posture becomes reframed, and our conversations with Him are transformed. The focus, tone, and even the intention of our prayers are redirected more into alignment with God's will and His priorities. Instead of offering a string of requests born out of disappointments and frustrations, we pause in His presence, and we *see* Him. Priscilla Shirer wrote in *Discerning the Voice of God*.

Let's now get to a quiet place and ask God a question that I know he wants to answer. Ask Him, God, why do You love me? Ask Him now; it doesn't have to be aloud. After all, He can read your mind. Ask and then listen. Wait for an answer. What did He say? I have put some room at the back pages of this book, jot down what He said to you.

Isn't God so good? The first time I asked, He said, "Because I made you beautiful." That was salve to a wound that had been festering thirty-plus years. To think back, it still is like a big bear hug from my one true love, Jesus. I am praying right now that you would just have the sweetest moment with your Savior. I hope you heard the loving words of the Almighty. He *is* salve for your soul, whatever it looks like for you.

I did this exercise with my son, Cash, one day while I was driving in the car. That is when he asks the best questions and we have the best conversations, just him and me driving in the car. He asked me, "How do you hear God's voice?" So I taught him about the still, small voice and said we could try to see whether God had something for him today. Cash closed his eyes and said, "God, why do You love me?" He sat silently for a minute, then smiled.

I asked, "What did you hear, buddy?"

He said, "'You are a sinner.'"

Huh? I was very confused by this and wanted to say in a mama-bear voice, *That's not God. That's the enemy.* But I said very calmly in my "I'm cool" voice, "Oh, okay, tell me how that made you feel." I was ready to combat the enemy's lies.

But Cash was glowing and said, "He loves me even though I make mistakes sometimes."

Wow! This came from my child, whose hardest thing was to admit fault. It's what God knows we are working on. I told him, "I will celebrate when you admit fault. It's good to learn from mistakes." So for God to tell him, "You are a sinner, but I died for you anyway, and I love you anyway," that was exactly what Cash needed to hear. I would have never been able to know that. Only God can speak to him so personally. My son didn't need to hear, "You're beautiful." He needed to hear, "You are forgiven." People cannot give you what you need; only your Savior can. And I know He is chasing after you. If you would just stop, listen, and turn to Him ... you will find Him.

Now if you didn't hear anything right now, that is okay too. Keep pressing into Him. Keep listening and looking for Him. He wants to show you who He is and who you are to Him. Maybe even ask someone else who is seasoned in prayer to help you open up the lines of communication. I needed to have someone help me get rid of my guilt and shame before I clearly heard the voice of God. Remember what the father of lies wants to talk about? Your past. He wants to lie and deceive you. Don't listen to that. What Father God wants more than anything is obedience, not sacrifice. He wants you to keep pressing into Him and obeying His word.

And Jesus answered, "You shall love the Lord your God with all your heart and with all your soul and with all your strength and with all your mind, and love your neighbor as yourself" (Luke 10:27 ESV).

Obedience is His love language. It is what we have to give Him back for all He has done for us. Love God and love people. This is His command to you. He tells us this in all four Gospels. Love God, love people.

But what about when people aren't very lovable? What then?

CHAPTER 8

The Pillar

Then he led them with the cloud by day
And all the night with a light of fire.
—Psalm 78:14

When I got married, people gave us all kinds of advice. Don't go to bed angry. Love is a choice. Communication is key. But I never really grasped the "You don't just marry the man. You marry the family" thing. Sure, at first everything was great. A true honeymoon phase. All families got along; we even spent our first Christmas all together—my mom and her husband, my dad and his wife, Nate's dad and his girlfriend, Nate's mom and her parents. We were all together under our roof for a Christmas celebration.

The other thing I wasn't prepared for was the melding of family traditions. On Easter, I grew up with the Easter basket full of the essentials: socks, underwear, toothbrush, Easter dress, and some candy. There were always bunny tracks throughout the house leading us to our prizes.

Nate's family was all about the candy, the little foiled chocolate eggs hidden all over the house and even the yard sometimes, followed by a basketful of sugar candy. No socks, no Easter "outfits," no toothbrushes, just candy.

Christmas proved to be just as different. One family gave tons of gifts, and the other family gave one gift to share as a couple. During our first Christmas as a married couple, we got a "shop vac" to share. Nate was excited. For me, it isn't about the quantity or money spent; it's about whether I feel seen. The joint shop vac didn't make me feel seen.

This story will give you a picture of where my heart was when it came to Christmas. Christmas was a time to give and receive gifts and a time to get all your divorced parents together for a very awkward day of eating, drinking, and gift opening. We didn't even have any kids at the time to break the awkwardness. Thankfully, we made it, all of us.

Time went on. I learned to split Christmas up, run to four different homes, and start new traditions as a family. But the mother-in-law and daughter-in-law relationship is tricky. There is a fine dance to be done. Nate has one brother and no sisters, so his mom is a "boy mom." She was the woman in their lives for decades. She was the one Nate went to the week before our first date to buy a new shirt, and then she helped him iron said shirt. She was the best cook on the planet, kept an immaculate house, and was my direct competition. I got mad at her because when she watched our oldest girl, Elliot, she did all our laundry. Isn't that rude? She obviously just wanted to tell Nate I wasn't doing a good job. She would keep a better house and always keep up with the laundry, right? As silly as this is, that is how I felt.

Once we got some ground rules down, she and I started to do okay. I wasn't as sensitive, and she respected the new role she was in. Then things started to get scary. Once we came home from a date night, and Nate's mom, Joan, and her mother, "GG" (Great-Grandma), were babysitting. They had Elliot and Cash in the backyard, playing on the swing set; they were all laughing and telling us about the fun they had that night.

Something was different about Joan; she was slurring her words—not horribly. But it was enough that we both noticed it and were very concerned. We didn't say anything that night; she left, and her slavery to prescription drug abuse started. Freedom was what we all wanted, but the drug kept her a slave for over ten years. We didn't know where to go with this battle.

The Israelites found themselves in an unknown place as well. They had been in slavery for four hundred years. Many generations had gone by, and all of them had known only slavery. They had never been free. They didn't know what to do with their new freedom or where to go.

God made it very simple on them. He was going to lead them. He was their guide. He was their GPS.

When Pharaoh let the people go, God didn't lead them by way of the land of the Philistines, although that was near. God said, "Lest the people change their minds when they see war and return to Egypt" (Exodus 13:17).

God saw that even though it would be a faster trip to go straight through the land of the Philistines, it would also be deadly. The Philistines meant war; they didn't mess around. God didn't want His people to leave slavery and head into a battle. God didn't want that for them. He knew they couldn't handle it and might even turn right around and run back to slavery.

Have you ever begged God to give you a straight path? Or said, "Why does this have to be such a long process? Why can't we just move right to the finish line fast?" "They moved from Succoth and encamped at Etham, on the edge of the wilderness" (Exodus 13:20).

Not only did God not lead them on the fastest path; He also led them to the wilderness. This doesn't seem right, does it? Like Moses and me, the people of God needed to have some training and faith building. How did He lead them? "And the Lord went before them by day in a pillar of cloud to lead them along the way, and by night in a pillar of fire to give them light, that they may travel by day and by night. The pillar of cloud by day and the pillar of fire by night did not depart from before the people" (Exodus 13:21–22).

Okay, let's try to wrap our heads around how this went down.

I mean seriously, this is pretty crazy. I hear people just gloss over this miracle all the time. Have you ever seen a pillar of cloud? I haven't. What would that look like? Blue skies everywhere but one pillar you can't get your arms around jutting straight up to the sky for all to see? Does that mean it was the only cloud? Otherwise how would they know which cloud to follow?

Then try to visualize how dark it must have been at night. No city lights to distort the stars. Pure darkness with a pillar of fire shooting up from the tent. That had to put any northern lights or Fourth of July fireworks show to shame. One giant pillar of fire to light the way. Wow! That cannot be explained away like a fluke of strange weather. This is an act of God, and they followed it. They followed the God-sized GPS, a cloud by day and fire by night.

If someone describes you as a pillar of strength, she's saying you're reliable and supportive, much like a pillar or column of a building that helps hold the structure up. The spelling of the word *pillar* looks like it has two pillars right at its center, holding the word up. *Pillar* is interchangeable with the word *column*, though you can't always use them in the same contexts. While a column and a pillar are both physical cylindrical structures, a column can also be the row running up and down on a chart, while a pillar is often someone or a thing considered a foundation or support. Someone indispensable to your company might be considered a pillar to the organization.

Who is the foundation and support of our faith? Whom are we to look to in times of need and plenty? Who will never leave us or forsake us? Nehemiah summarizes what God the Father did for the Israelites.

> You saw the suffering of our ancestors in Egypt; you heard their cry at the Red Sea. You sent signs and wonders against Pharaoh, against all his officials and all the people of his land, for you knew how arrogantly the Egyptians treated them.

You made a name for yourself, which remains to this day. You divided the sea before them, so that they passed through it on dry ground, but you hurled their pursuers into the depths, like a stone into mighty waters. By day you lead them with a pillar of cloud, and by night with a pillar of fire to give them light on the way they were to take. You came down on Mount Sinai; you spoke to them from heaven. You gave them regulations and laws that are just and right, and decrees and commands that are good. You made known to them your holy Sabbath and gave them commands, decrees and laws through your servant Moses. In their hunger you gave them bread from heaven and in their thirst you brought them water from the rock; you told them to go in and take possession of the land you had sworn with uplifted hand to give them. (Nehemiah 9:9–15)

God gave them the land. He provided the way and the food and water. He guided them along the path, but they didn't always keep their eyes fixed on Him.

Years later, Jesus came to the earth to be a pillar of faith for us. He walked with the disciples for three years, teaching them and showing them He was not only fully man but fully God. They could physically touch Him, hold Him, and ask any questions they had. Peter was wonderful at this. I love Peter. He made many mistakes, asked stupid questions, and had a love for the Lord like few others.

One day Jesus sent the boys off in a boat to do some ministry, and Jesus was going to catch up with them after He finished speaking to the Father. They were a long way off, but Jesus was on the mountaintop praying, so He could see they were struggling. The storm had really stirred the waters. The boat was slamming into the waves. The Bible tells the story so well. Let's read it.

Jesus made the disciples get into the boat and go on ahead of him to the other side, while he dismissed the crowd. After he had dismissed them, he went up on a mountainside by himself to pray. Later that night, he was there alone, and the boat was already a considerable distance from land, buffeted by the waves because the wind was against it. Shortly before dawn Jesus went out to them, walking on the lake. When the disciples saw him walking on the lake, they were terrified. "It's a ghost," they said, and cried out in fear. But Jesus said to them: "Take courage! It is I. Don't be afraid." "Lord, if it's you," Peter replied, "tell me to come to you on the water." "Come," he said. Then Peter got down out of the boat, walked on the water and came toward Jesus. But when he saw the wind, he was afraid and, beginning to sink, cried out, "Lord, save me!" Immediately Jesus reached out his hand and caught him. (Matthew 14:22–31)

I love this story. I am going to focus on Peter for a minute. First of all, he left the crowd and went out into the waters, into the unknown, just because Jesus had told him to. Great faith, right? Then the waves and wind started up, and he held onto the boat for dear life. Thankfully he still had his fishing buddies with him so he wasn't alone. Then fear came. A ghost was walking up to the boat. Only a second went by before his friend, Jesus, reassured him that it was Him walking on water. Peter asked for proof. "If it is you, Lord, tell me to come to you on the water."

Then Peter walked on the water.

He did so because Jesus had called him to it. He called Peter out on the water, and he went. Talk about faith. I cry out because God has called me to write a book and speak to women about him. I'm scared to do so. I think Peter was scared as he stepped both feet out of the boat, but he did it. Yes, he then saw the wind and the waves, and he sank. He sank hard and fast, but he first walked on water.

My story seems so lame compared to this story, but I still relate. Even though this is the middle of the book, it is actually toward the end of writing for me. I added this chapter later. I got out of the boat, stepped on the water, and wrote most of the book. Then I saw the wind and waves, and I started sinking.

I took my eyes off Jesus and started to rely on things of this world for comfort, and the production of this book came to a screeching halt. I started thinking, *What if I am more like a Peter than I thought?* Faith is strong one minute, and then suddenly my faith is sinking. What if it doesn't feel like I am being led? Where are my cloud and fire to follow? I can't see this through all the striving, comparing, and tacos. Like my mother-in-law and Peter, I believe they both thought their faith was enough to stay above the water. Maybe they thought believing in Jesus was enough. Maybe they thought they could take their eyes off Jesus and still walk on the water. Perhaps I thought so too.

My mother-in-law's freedom looked like cancer. She was taken home to freedom five weeks after she heard the c-word. Her going was beautiful, all her family by her side. Nate asked her whether she wanted to see Jesus, and she closed her eyes and repeated, "Looking forward to it ... looking forward to it."

I want to take after her and look forward to Jesus right now, not with a terminal disease, not because I'm at my last straw, but because He is here, waiting for me to just perform for Him alone. Drop all the distractions and look to Jesus.

Lord, help me to have the strength to look and follow You alone. Thank You for being my pillar, which I can depend on, lean on, and jump out onto the scary waters with. You are right beside me. Amen.

CHAPTER 9

Water Walls

Then Moses stretched out his hand over the sea;
and the Lord swept the sea back by a strong east wind
all night and turned the sea into dry land,
so the waters were divided.

—Exodus 14:21

This year I have been walking through Exodus with our homeschool co-op. I have seen these words come to life not only in my heart but also in the heart of the children. I have seen them take root in the hearts of *my* children. When I was reading chapter 14 with our eight-year-old, Millie, she said, "Oh, yeah, God made a hallway with water walls for the people to walk through." Let me think about that for a minute. A hallway … with water walls? "Ha! Yes, honey, I guess He did." Oh, to have the eyes of a child! She saw it so plainly. It wasn't even strange to her to think about a hallway with water walls going through the middle of the sea. At what age is it that we start seeing things with skeptical eyes? When does our childlike faith change to doubt and uncertainty?

The Israelites had just been freed from Egypt. They went door to door and asked for all the Egyptians' stuff. The crazy thing is, the people gave all their stuff to them. They also saw all the plagues pass over them. The last one literally did. In the last plague God brought upon the people for Egypt, their firstborn child would be killed if they didn't obey God's voice. He wanted them to listen only to Him. He told them, "If you want your first born to live, I must be your only audience. Listen to My words." He spoke the words through Moses and Aaron. "Don't look to the customs of the people around you. Don't ask your neighbor what to do. Listen to *Me!*"

Moses said, "Thus says the Lord, 'about midnight I am going out into the midst of Egypt, and all the firstborn in the land of Egypt shall die, from the firstborn of Pharaoh who sits on his throne, even to the firstborn of the slave girl who is behind the millstones; all the first born cattle as well. Moreover, there shall be a great cry in all the land of Egypt, such as there has never been before and such as shall never be again'" (Exodus 11:5–6).

"All the firstborn of Egypt's people will die on this night," God said through Moses. "Everyone from Pharaoh, to the slaves, even to the Egyptian animals will feel the wrath of me this night.

"BUT against any of the sons of Israel a dog will not even bark, whether against man or beast, so that you may understand how the Lord makes a distinction between Egypt and Israel" (Exodus 11:7)

To set the scene, this terrible awful thing was happening to the Egyptians. People were screaming over the loss of their loved ones. Blood-curdling screaming passed all over because every household was affected by this plague, but the Israelites' neighborhood was silent. Not even a dog barked. I cannot wrap my head around this. How does this happen? Why did this have to happen?

It had to happen *so* you and I may understand how the Lord makes a distinction between Egypt and Israel.

God wanted the Egyptians to look around and say, "Hey, why aren't the Israelites being affected by these plagues? Why are they always protected? Yeah, their lives are really hard (being slaves and all), but why are they so joyful and peaceful?" God was showing that His people were set apart, distinct from all others.

God was very clear on the directions for safety. They were given instructions of what to do. Have you ever been given instructions on what to do? If you ever bought anything from IKEA, you received a manual of instructions on how to build the shelf, dresser, or table. The instructions are never as simple as you would think. When I look at the stunning piece of furniture in the store, I don't expect to have to take a week off work to put the thing together. I don't expect to need marriage counseling when I look at the dining room table and six chairs in the store. Anyway, I don't always do the best with instructions. I think *I* know best how to read them, and my husband somehow sees them completely differently. In his defense, he is in construction and reads blueprints every day and all day long. Why is it that I still think I know more than he does? I don't even know why I am admitting this to you right now.

Back to the instructions. "Take some of the blood and put it on the two doorposts and the lintel of the houses in which they eat it" (Exodus 12:7).

This is the main instruction we remember. There were other specifics of the process, but basically if the people did this, they were saved from the plague. How likely do you think you would be to do this? It had most likely been years that they have endured these plagues against their "gods," and now there was a threat against their oldest child's life. I have to think all of them would have taken precautions at this point. Sadly, they still didn't choose to trust and follow God.

"Pharaoh rose up in the night, he and all the servants and all the Egyptians. And there was a great cry in Egypt, for there was not a house where someone was not dead. Then he summoned Moses and Aaron by night and said, 'Up, go out from among my people, both you and the people of Israel; go, serve the Lord, as you have said. Take your flocks and your herds, as you have said, and be gone, and bless me also!'" (Exodus 12:31–32).

This is heartbreaking! I cannot help but see what that looks like now. First, I want to remind you that the covenant Israel was under was an if/then covenant. *If* they did good, *then* good things happened. *If* they did bad things, *then* bad things happened. You get the point. Now, because of Jesus's death and resurrection, we have grace. The free gift is something we just have to choose to open, but still so many don't make that choice. How heartbreaking!

After I learned how to discern God's voice, I asked Him to replace shame and abandonment with a blessing. After all, He is a good father who knows how to give good gifts. I prayed and heard *joy* and *freedom*. How awesome is that? Yes, I will take joy and freedom as opposed to shame and abandonment? Any day! But then He. Kept. Going.

I also got *order* and *discipline* ... What? Those aren't blessings, are they? Okay, let's keep going and revisit that later. And He kept going.

Lastly, I was given an audience of One. "Blessed be the God and Father of our Lord Jesus Christ, who has blessed us with every spiritual blessing in the heavenly places in Christ, just as he chose us in him before the foundation of the world" (Ephesians 1:3–4).

Joy and freedom I totally understood and were excited about, but the rest of these ... I don't know. And why so many blessings? But I was willing to continue. Next, I wanted to know when the father of lies would tell me the lies of shame and abandonment. So I closed my eyes and asked and listened, but this time He gave me a visual memory.

I was about five years old. I was in my parents' big red house. In the kitchen I would stand under the countertop or breakfast bar that jutted over the stools. There my brother and I ate our Wheaties.

I was under the counter and looking straight ahead and to the left. There wasn't anyone there; I was alone. But then my mom was there on the phone, laughing. I couldn't make out what she was saying, but she seemed happy. I don't think she even knew I was in the room. Then my dad came into the room, and he was mad. They started arguing. I don't know what about, but I was still hidden under the counter alone.

During my prayer session, Pam kept asking me where Jesus was. I didn't see Him anywhere. I could see only my mom and dad arguing. They had my entire attention and focus. She encouraged me to look around everywhere. Just then I turned to my right, and right there beside me was ...

Before I tell you who or what was beside me, I want to revisit the Israelites. After ten different horrible plagues on the Egyptians, the king finally let the people go. "The Lord was going before them in pillar of cloud by day to lead them on the way, and a pillar of fire by night to give them light, that they might travel by day and by night. He did not take away the pillar of cloud by day, nor the pillar of fire by night, from before the people" (Exodus 13:21–22).

He will never leave you or forsake you. God gave them a GPS in the form of a cloud and fire.

God led them right to the perfect place, the beach. I love the beach. Who doesn't? We love to go "shelling" (I'm not sure whether that is a verb) on Sanibel Island, Florida, as often as we can. The hidden treasures wash up on shore every evening and morning on high tide. It is a glorious treasure hunt. I wonder what people did when they saw the waters.

The Red Sea is actually a saltwater lake but of vast dimensions. It is a sea full of wildlife, sea creatures, and shells. I wonder, *When they got to the beach, were they in wonder of their freedom and beauty set before them?* I was. I love to sit alone with God and be in awe of the beauty around me. I could see so much more beauty now that I was free than I ever had before. But then the "world wave" came. You know how this could happen? You are sitting and minding your own business, worshipping the risen Savior, and bam! An army shows up at your door, a world wave.

A literal army showed up at the Israelites' beachfront picnic. They were busy "shelling" while the Egyptian husbands came home and weren't altogether too happy. Nor was Pharaoh. God's hand was all over this again. Exodus 14:4 says, "Thus I will harden Pharaoh's heart, and he will chase after them; I will be honored through Pharaoh and all his army and the Egyptians will know that I am the Lord."

Sometimes the world wave comes because our enemy needs to know Jesus is Lord. Then we have a choice on how we are going to react to it. This is how the people of Israel reacted after they were set free, given all they could need. They were safe at the shore with their God overhead in a pillar of cloud. "As Pharaoh drew near, the sons of Israel looked, and behold, the Egyptians were marching after them, and they became very frightened; so they cried out to the Lord" (Exodus 14:10).

Okay, this makes sense. Pharaoh was coming at them with six hundred chariots, plus all the other chariots of Egypt. All his horsemen were going to overtake them at the sea. So it would be natural to get scared in our humanness. It is natural to be afraid when your house is being foreclosed on and all your earthly possessions are being hauled away by the trailer load. It would make sense to get scared and ask God why. "I just gave my life over to You, like ten minutes ago. Why the suffering? Why the embarrassment? I thought I was following Your lead." I understand the Israelites. They followed the cloud; they did as God had said. Why the attack from an army of my enemies? I'm with them so far.

Verse 11 says, "Then they say to Moses, 'Is it because there were no graves in Egypt that you have taken us away to die in the wilderness? Why have you [Moses] dealt with us in this way, bringing us out of Egypt? [blame] Is this not the word that we spoke to you in Egypt, saying, "leave us alone that we may serve the Egyptians?" For it would have been better for us to serve the Egyptians than to die in the wilderness'"

They desired slavery.

The Israelites' cycle isn't too different from ours sometimes.

1. Look and be scared.
2. Cry out to the Lord.
3. Blame.
4. Desire slavery.

I have sadly run this cycle too many times to count. Right after we accepted Christ, when our house and all our things were being taken, we looked around and got *scared*. What were we going to do? Where would we live? What would we drive? What would the neighbors think? What would our friends and family say?

Then we (may have) pointed fingers at one another a time or two. Blame. *Why aren't you better at paying the bills? Why don't you just work harder at work and make more money?* (We were both working at that time.) *How could you let it get this bad? Why are you spending all our money?*

Then the absolute heartbreak happens; once you start on this cycle, it will end here. If we weren't followers of Christ, we could cheat on our taxes, work for cash "under the table," do hair without a license in our home for extra money, or fill in your blank. If only_____then. Heartbreak, the moment it hits you that you are desiring the very slavery God has freed you from.

There is another way, God said through Moses.

"'Do not fear! Stand by and see the salvation of the Lord which He will accomplish for you today; for the Egyptians whom you have seen today, you will never see them again forever. The Lord will fight for you while you keep silent.' Then the Lord said to Moses, 'Why are you crying out to Me? Tell the sons of Israel to move forward'" (Exodus 14:13–14).

God says:

1. Do not fear 280 times in the Bible.
2. Stand by and wait expectantly.
3. See and look for what the Lord is doing.
4. Move and take action.

I believe an entire book could be written just on these points, but for now here is my example. At the end of 2010, Nate and I accepted Christ. Six months later we packed our boxes of what we had left and moved from our beautiful two-story home and into a small town house closer to our new church family. Once we knew we were losing our house, thankfully we had just given over our lives to Jesus and were living in our new freedom.

1. We didn't fear what was next. We had peace beyond all understanding.
2. We waited for God to move. We trusted He would.
3. We watched as He changed the foreclosure to a short sale.
4. We moved … literally.

The first night we were in the town house, I sat at our same kitchen table, now in a new space, and wrote about how thankful I was to still have all that was important. All that mattered. I still had my family and my God.

The prophet Nehemiah wrote in 9:19, "You, in Your great *compassion*, did not forsake them in the wilderness; the pillar of cloud did not leave them by day, to guide them on their way, nor the pillar of fire by night, to light for them the way in which they were to go" (emphasis added).

The Lord said to Moses, "Why do you cry to me? Tell the people of Israel to go forward. Lift up your staff and stretch out your hand over the sea and divide it, that the people of Israel may go through the sea on dry ground" (Exodus 14:15).

God told Moses, "Move. You do it. I gave you My authority. Now use it. Free my people." God was there with Moses in his scariest moment. Armies stacked him and his people, shouting at him that he had messed up badly. God was still so patient. He was still there, ready to cheer him on. That's where I was, under the counter. My parents were fighting, I didn't feel *seen* at all. I thought I was alone to handle this.

But I wasn't.

Continued Foreshadow

She was so focused on what was happening in front of her, with her parents arguing, that she *couldn't* look anywhere else. She was frozen, fixed on the argument, unable to see anything else. Did someone say "divorce"? What did that mean? The sound of the word was serious and final, sounded like a dagger to the heart, to all their hearts.

When she shook her head in disbelief and confusion, something on the other side of her caught her eye. Slowly she turned her head. Right there, sitting under the counter with her, was Jesus.

I don't know how she knew what His name was, but she knew His was Jesus. On His face was pure delight. He was delighting in *her*. She couldn't keep her eyes off Him. And His eyes were fixed on her. He never even noticed her parents fighting. He didn't seem like He was there to do anything but delight in *her*.

He told her He wanted to set her free and give her joy. He talked about things she didn't fully understand, like order and disciple. He talked about living for an audience of One. She didn't know what all that meant, but she knew she would go wherever He went.

Jesus told the little girl He wanted to bring her to His Father. She couldn't wait. She said yes immediately.

It was as if she were in a dream. He took her to a wide-open space, with bright yellow and white light all around her. There weren't any walls or barriers, yet she felt completely free and safe. Everything seemed to make sense, and all of her worry and concern faded away the moment they arrived. Jesus stood there, holding her hand the whole time like her friend and protector. He was safety and security. He was *love*.

The little girl was so free and joyful that she started to dance. She had never danced before, but she twirled and twirled like she was on the stage of a Broadway musical.

Her Savior, her Lord, her God was her audience of One.

I looked to the right, and under the counter with me was *Jesus*! I could see Him now that I was looking for him. I wasn't distracted by my surroundings. I found him right there beside me, and I was mesmerized. "He brought me out into a broad place; he rescued me, because he delighted in me" (Psalm 18:19).

The only way I can describe His face is *pure delight*.

Delight is *not* a word I think I have ever used in a sentence up until that day. It just wasn't in my vocabulary, but on that fall day, I experienced what it felt like to be delighted in. Suddenly nothing that was going on with my parents mattered to me. It was as if they had left and Jesus had brought me to another universe just to snuggle with me and *delight* in me.

> De·light: please (someone) greatly, please greatly, charm, enchant, captivate, entrance, thrill.

Oh … kay … I will take the Savior of the world captivated, enchanted, moved, and greatly pleased with me *any day*! Those words I can feel and touch and hold onto. They are straight out of a fairy tale, and I was right in the middle of one. Right under my kitchen counter, having the God of the universe thrilled with me, I found Him *delighting* in *me*.

What the enemy tried to use as a platform for destruction the Lord restored.

Disclaimer: *Do not* think this message was given to me and me alone. This isn't *my* story; this is *our* story. God has been very clear to me on that. This gift, this vision, isn't for me alone. It is for you. And hold on because we're not even close to being done. He has so much more to show you.

> From the very first day, we were there, taking it all in-we heard it with our own ears, saw it with our own eyes, verified it with our own hands. The Word of Life appeared right before our eyes; we saw it happen! And now we're telling you in most sober prose that what we witnessed was, incredibly, this: The infinite Life of God himself took shape before us. We saw it, we heard it, and now we're telling you so you can experience it along with us, this experience of communion with the Father and his Son, Jesus Christ. (1 John 1:1–3 MSG)

I was in beautiful communion with Jesus under the counter. I really wanted to name this book "Jesus is under the counter" just to remind us that He is everywhere with us. No matter if you are at work, at home, hiding in a closet, crying, or in your darkest moments of life, Jesus is with you. He is even under the counter.

So Jesus and I were chillin' under the counter.

Then I asked Him to bring me to the Father. After all, the only way to the Father is through the Son. This seems crazy to me as I write this three years later, that I literally asked Jesus to bring me to Father God. Who does that? But right on, Trisha. You go, ask, and you shall receive.

Immediately I could see I was in a great, open expanse; bright yellow light was almost a fog all around me, but I could see clearly. I was saying things like, "There are *no* walls, no barriers. Nothing is separating me from the Father." I of course didn't "see" Father God, but there was no question in my mind that He was there and loving me like I had never felt love before. It was love that was heavy and yet gentle, explosive but still. I wanted to jump up and down and also lie flat on my face before Him.

Jesus was right beside me, holding my little hand and smiling *still* with pure delight. (I know I keep using the same word *delight*, but no other word comes close to giving it justice.)

Suddenly, I was a little older, and I was twirling.

At this point, tears were running, streaming down my face. It was an ugly cry, to say the least. So of course Pam asked me what was happening. Remember, I was still in a guided prayer meeting. I told her I was dancing (I am not a dancer, by the way), twirling for the King of all kings, Lord of lords, the Creator of all, my all and all. I was dancing.

The Father was telling me *this* was all He wanted from me. He and me. No walls, no distractions, no barriers, no one else. Just Him and me. And all I was doing was performing for my audience of One. It didn't matter whether I was the smartest, prettiest, skinniest, funniest, best cook, best housekeeper; or whether I had the best car, house, or toys. *All* that mattered was that I was performing for my audience of One: my King, my Savior, my Lord, my "Audient"!

So I went back under the counter with Jesus, and I had complete peace. Again, a place the enemy had used to plant a seed of destruction and unworthiness was now my safe haven. It was my security, my meeting place with God.

CHAPTER 10

Freedom

Over and over Scripture suggests this: God,
our Maker, Savior, Redeemer, and King wants interaction
with His prized creation even in all our flaws
and frailties and doubts and failures.
And not just interaction. He wants engagement.
And not just engagement. He wants intimacy.

—Beth Moore [9]

I just came off the most crazy, surreal, incredible experience of my life. What was I supposed to do now with my new freedom?

I'm sure you have gotten this by now, but if not, I'm going to tell you. I am not a quiet person. This wasn't going to stay with just me. I wasn't going to be the only one to know about this newfound freedom. I'm pretty sure on the way home I called my husband while he was framing a house, standing on a roof or a plank or something, and I puked this amazing encounter with God on him. He, I'm sure, was engaged and asked tons of questions and was changed because of it.

That's not really how it works in my house. For some reason I don't get his full attention when I call in the middle of him working. Although I know he would love to have the time and

---

[9] The Quest - Study Journal: An Excursion Toward Intimacy with God, 2017

mind space for one of my deep life-changing conversations, that doesn't always happen while he's literally balancing on a two-story roof truss. This time for this encounter I was able to sit for a minute and soak it all in.

Later that night I was able to share with him what God had shown me, and he was able to ask questions that he had and let it all sink in. My husband, Nate, wasn't the only one I told. Like I said earlier, I knew immediately this was a message of great importance and soon learned it would span oceans, languages, demographics, and any and all places where God wanted to send it.

Although it was an extremely intimate time with my Savior, He wants to free His people. Do you remember back at the beginning of this book? I related myself to Moses while doubting the plan God had set before me? What else did God say to Moses? He said, "Go, set My people free!"

As I am writing this, it gets me so excited, scared, awe inspired, and amazed at the God I serve, we serve. At this point in your life, if you haven't given your life over to this amazing God, I want you to know you can do so in an instant, not with any special words or ceremony. But the intimate God I met under the counter is ready and chasing after you. Whether you are a long way off or just hanging out on top of the fence, He is there to catch you. He wants you, dirty laundry and all.

One of my favorite songs is called "O Come to the Altar" by Elevation Music. I had the privilege and honor of recently speaking at a young women's retreat at the girls-led worship. A big sigh and pulling back tears when I think about it. Even more than that, my thirteen-year-old daughter was one of the leaders. (Gah! Blinking away tears.) Even more than that, all these young girls sang like angels.

Side note: recently we went to family camp. As we were singing, our eight-year-old daughter stood on the chair behind me and leaned forward onto me with her little arms around my neck. As she sang, her mouth was right by my ear. She makes a joyful noise, I tell you. Sometimes she will be downstairs singing, and I honestly get a little scared that someone is hurt until I realize it's just Millie singing. But this day, as she was hugging my neck and singing to the God who had created her, I'm sure I had never heard anything more beautiful. Her little voice would crack and squeak here and there like a VeggieTales track.

Tears streamed down my face at the beauty of her broken voice crying out to her God. I can't help but feel the joy God must have when one of His children cries out to Him in his or her brokenness. Whether it's a broken heart or a broken voice, He *loves* it all; He wants it all.

The weekend with the youth girls wasn't like a "joyful noise." This was the clouds opening and the angels signing in three-part harmony. These young women could sing! So imagine me getting ready to speak and standing in the back. To be more accurate, I was basically lying on the floor facedown. This is how some of the song goes ("O Come to the Altar" by Elevation Worship).

> Are you hurting and broken within?
> Overwhelmed by the weight of your sin?
> Jesus is calling
> Have you come to the end of yourself
> Do you thirst for a drink from the well?
> Jesus is calling
>
> O come to the altar
> The Father's arms are open wide
> Forgiveness was bought with
> The precious blood of Jesus Christ
>
> Leave behind your regrets and mistakes
> Come today there's no reason to wait
> Jesus is calling
> Bring your sorrows and trade them for joy

From the ashes a new life is born
Jesus is calling

O come to the altar
The Father's arms are open wide
Forgiveness was bought with
The precious blood of Jesus Christ[10]

Jesus is calling! He is calling you. He is calling your children. He is calling your parents and the friend who feels unworthy. The neighbor who feels unseen. The coworker who just can't seem to get it together. Jesus is calling. He wants us all to be free of our burdens, regrets, and mistakes. We are free if we just let Him take them.

"My yoke is easy. My burden is light," He tells us.

The week after meeting Jesus under the counter in Bible study, I was charged to divide my life into fifths and ask God where He was in each section of my life. That week happened to be the section that involved my twenties. Another (not-so-great) emotion that set in immediately was fear. What if I open myself up to shame and abandonment again? How can I stay free? What if I am just on a high and this won't last? What if I just "made all this up"? When I was reading my Bible study that week and the writer asked me to revisit my twenties, I was nervous.

I didn't want to think about all the drinking, partying, and make-out sessions I did in my early twenties. You know those cute little signs or sayings people post on Facebook that have a woman in the 1950s drinking a glass of wine? It says things like, "I have to go. The kids chewed through their straps" or something like that. About a year after I gave my life over to Christ, a "friend" from my past posted one on her wall. It said something like "Enough with all your spiritual Facebook posts. I knew you when you a

---

[10] O Come to the Altar, Elevation Worship–©copyright

floozy" Deep breath. Okay, if our memories aren't already vivid and condemning enough, others will jump in to remind us of our sins.

Sadly, this wasn't the first time something like this had happened. The night I graduated from high school, we all were escorted to an "overnighter" filled with games, a hair salon (where I got my hair done into a fancy french twist (it was the '90s), and lots of food and candy. The walls were lined with paper for us to write memories or cute, little notes to each other. Of course, I am scouring the paper, looking for some love declaration or sweet note to me from someone, anyone; and then there it was in black and white. Someone had written a word, describing me, that was not loving and was not beautiful, but it was sexual and degrading.

And they couldn't even spell the word right. At the time I didn't know it was spelled wrong. Remember, I was terrible at spelling; he must have had the same teachers. Needless to say, the rest of my night was in the bathroom, makeup running down my face. I ripped that french twist out. Why bother? My friends ran around like Sherlock Holmes, trying to find the person who would do that. I had one boyfriend in tenth grade with whom I made a huge mistake and got pregnant. That evidence was the ammunition. Because of that, I was tagged with that name. I didn't even deserve to have it spelled correctly.

These were the things I was afraid to bring to mind and start the spiral of shame again. I put it off all week. I mustered up enough confidence to finally start praying about this part of my life. In an attempt to combat all my fears, I thought I would just ask Jesus where He had been during this shameful time of my life. After my prayer session with Pam, I knew He loved me so much and wanted what was best for me. I felt I could ask him where He had been during my *greatest* sin. I was by myself this time. I didn't have the help of someone to guide me in prayer this time. I figured I already knew how it would go.

I thought Jesus would be over in the corner, cringing because of His great love for me. He would be saying things like, "Please don't do that, baby girl. I love you so much. That just isn't good for you." Are you picturing the scene?

Well, that isn't how it went, not at all. Yes, I saw myself in the ugliness of my shameful sin (enjoying it), and I looked around, and there was Jesus, just like I knew He would be, always will be. He will never leave me or forsake me. His face was nothing like I thought it would be. He was in pure delight of me, saying things like, "I love you, baby girl. You are *so* loved and *so* wanted!" He looked at me with delight: no shame, no condemnation, no projected guilt but delight. My audience of One was delighting in *me* ... how is that possible? He didn't look at the sin I was in because He *hates* sin. He died, rose again, and defeated sin! He was delighting in me: His child, daughter, princess, and daughter of the King, who was white as snow. Why? Because He had paid it all! All of it was done! I couldn't do, say, or want to do anymore to make me clean. He did it all. Period.

So what was left?

Freedom.

I am now free from any memory that would bubble to the surface. I am free from any reminder on social media. I am free from any future temptation I would fall into. I was free last week when I ran into the guy who wrote that terrible word on the wall during my last day of high school. I was free to enjoy my dinner with my family and even tell my husband the story on the way home. As I told the story, I felt bad for the guy. He was a teenager who had told a bad joke. He has apologized to me, but I still see the regret in his eyes. Our words are powerful, but Jesus paid it all. I am free! Jesus didn't pay it all just for me.

> Oh what a savior
> Isn't He wonderful?
> Sing hallelujah, Christ is risen
> Bow down before Him

For He is Lord of all
Sing Hallelujah, Christ is risen
The Father's arms are open wide
Forgiveness was bought with
The precious blood of Jesus Christ

Then the song ends with this:

Bear your cross as you wait for the crown
Tell the world of the treasure you found.
[11]("O Come to the Altar," Elevation Worship)

Read this testimony of my friend, Amy, who carried her cross.

Like Trisha, I did an RTF healing or deliverance prayer session. We worked on feelings of being unworthy, orphan spirit, rejection, failure, not being taken care of or protected, and so forth.

The memory He brought me to was not anything I thought I needed healing from, so that was a bit confusing at the start. It was probably one of the most idyllic times of my life. I was around the age of four or five, and we lived in Buffalo, Minnesota. I was a tomboy with a capital *T*. I loved to go explore and take walks, looking for treasures (rocks, agates, butterflies, frogs, flowers, grasshoppers, and so forth). All day long!

The memory started off with me sitting behind my bed by myself. I liked to hide and spend time alone. My bed was in the corner of my room, so there was a perfect little gap between my headboard and the wall. I loved hanging

---

[11] O come to the altar, Elevation Worship–©copyright

out there. I was confused why Jesus picked this memory to heal because I was content there, but then I realized a whole laundry list of emotions that weren't content or happy.

At first I thought I was alone, but then I saw Jesus all scrunched up behind the bed with me. I asked Him if He would take all the negative feelings I was processing back behind the bed, and He said yes.

All of a sudden we were outside in nature with a stream running next to us. Jesus had His arms full of all my emotional baggage. Then He tossed each emotion one by one into the moving stream and washed them away. Then I asked if He had anything to give me in return. Jesus walked up to the little four-year-old me and handed me a huge, heavy cross and told me to carry my cross. Huh? What? Well, that seemed odd, impossible, full of Christianese, religious spirit and not very kind or loving, especially for a child. I felt confused and disheartened. I thought that it didn't seem very "Jesus-y." I asked Him, "How am I supposed to carry this?" Instantly, He picked it up and strapped it to His back like a teeny, tiny backpack with nothing in it. He then grabbed my hand, and we went on a treasure walk, and He skipped along right beside me playfully, pointing out all of the treasures He had put along my path that were just for me. He wasn't burdened by my cross or even seemed like it affected Him at all. Unlike if I were to try to even lift it, let alone drag it with me throughout my day. He showed me that He was always with me on my walks, laying out His treasures for me to find as I explored. "How does this apply to me as an adult, Lord?" He said, "The exact same way." As long as I walk hand in hand alongside Him, He will bear my burdens and carry my cross if I trust Him and continue to be in His presence as we walk together, and He will be pointing out all the treasures He has planned and laid out for me along the way. I have never imagined Jesus like this before He showed me this vision. He always seemed so holy and unattainable and far away. It makes me weep and my heart leap out of my chest to think He could possibly want to walk with me so closely, sweetly, and be so invested in me that He actually wants to

A. Carry my cross;
B. Hold my hand;
C. Set before me so many treasures.

And He is excited to point them out to me! That equals freedom.

As I (Amy) ponder and process this vision that Jesus so graciously has given me, I see many things that bless me. He took my false religious spirit of Him being so far away and too holy to be with and utterly destroyed it. Instead of the feeling that someone was with me, watching over me from a very far-off place, He shows up smack dab in the journey with me, holding my hand—walking with me in the heat of the day, with beads of sweat on His brow, burrs scratching in the dirt and grass, picking up rocks, trying to avoid the itch weed as we pick flowers and peer at gorgeous butterflies. All the while He is bearing the burden of my cross. It seems to not even hinder Him in any way as we rejoice in the treasures of His marvelous world. I find it beautiful, a beauty that only Jesus can give you. He chose to use such a stark contrast as asking a four-year-old to carry his or her cross versus showing me a vision of me as a full-grown adult and being told to carry my cross. It would be something I would have *struggled* to do. I would have felt fully capable; in my own strength and effort I would have grunted, yanked, and pulled as my hands got sweaty and sore from my own efforts to obey. And my muscles would cramp and grow increasingly weak from my work and attempt to drag this enormous beast of burden throughout my day. You know I am right. We all have forgotten to lean into our biggest asset because we are determined to do it on our own.

I then think of how beaten, bloody, and broken Jesus was when He was told to carry His cross to the place He was to be crucified. He kept falling and stumbling under the weight of it and due to the beaten-down, broken state of His physical body. What if what I do to beat myself up emotionally and mentally were transferred to the physical part of my body? I bet I would appear flogged just as Jesus was after His physical assault. That is why Jesus used my younger self to show me I needed to ask Him how I was supposed to carry my cross because He knew I would see it as utterly impossible with my age, size, and strength as a child. My child self was okay with Him carrying it. But now as an adult, there would be no way that I would ask Him or anyone else to carry my cross or my burdens that I alone am responsible for creating, even though I have also beaten myself up so horrendously that it is physically impossible for me to even drag the weight of my sins a few feet. Jesus was sinless, yet He was required to carry His cross until He couldn't. Jesus is clearly willing to carry and bear our burdens daily for us. That is exactly why He became flesh, lived a sinless life, died, and rose again. I am worthy, I am loved, I am able to go for a stroll with Jesus anytime I want. I can talk with Him, love Him, and ask for help and allow Him to help.

I am in love with this story of freedom. This is the privilege of the cross. Jesus doesn't expect us to carry our burdens. He wants to do this for us. All we have to do is walk with Him hand and hand. He longs to show us all the treasures He has laid out for us *while* He does the heavy lifting. That's freedom.

Our fears, shame, regrets, all the ugly words said about and to us are all nailed to the cross He is carrying for us. All we need to do is walk with Him and be amazed. That's freedom.

CHAPTER 11

Joy

Do not be grieved, for
the Joy of the Lord is my strength.
—Nehemiah 8:10

Happy.

That is one of my least favorite words. "Do what makes you happy." "Follow your heart." These sayings drive me crazy. I'm sorry, but the Lord doesn't care if you are happy; that is never the goal. Does He want to give you the desires of your heart if you are His follower? Yes. Does He want you to be content in all circumstances? Yes. Full of joy? Yes, but He isn't out to make you happy. Stick with me if you are feeling offended and scared.

Happiness is what we hear on social media or *think* is what we are supposed to get in a spouse or our kids. Happiness is at Disney World and fairy-tale stories. But happiness is gone when hard times come. You are struggling in your marriage; you're not happy. Your kids are disobedient; you're not happy. You don't get the promotion; you're not happy. You're having a bad hair day; you're not happy. Why do we strive and toil for happiness if it can fall apart the instant things don't go our way? Why then do we plan our lives, marriages, relationships, and jobs around happiness?

It seems like the moment I accepted Christ or He called me

to Himself (semantics), I ruffled a lot of feathers around me. I touched on this earlier. I just couldn't keep quiet about Him. I was so amazed by the freedom and joy I was experiencing in Christ that I inserted Him into any conversation. How's the weather? Jesus saves! What's for lunch? Do you know Jesus loves you?

"I would like three layers cut in my hair, please."

Hairstylists will be with me on this; normally I want to answer, "I cannot put three layers in your hair, not two, not seven layers. I can cut layers in your hair, but I cannot put a number to how many." *But* instead now I said, "Do you know I have been saved? Are you a Christ follower?" I couldn't help it.

Thankfully, for my professional career, I left the salon to stay home and pour life into my kids. They couldn't reject my new joy. Unfortunately some people surprisingly were turned off by this approach. This still baffles me (wink, wink).

The hardest thing I went through during those first years was the rejection of my very best friend. Nicole and I went to high school together. We had the same friend groups but really didn't connect one on one until we were in our twenties. We went through all the great, wonderful, adventurous times ... and the hard things that happen when you are first out on your own. We traveled together, laughed about stupid stuff, cried over breakups, danced into the wee hours together, made vats of tuna casserole, and ate it together at two o'clock in the morning. We were engaged and married in the same year. We both had baby girls first, and then the boys came eleven days apart from one another. We did life together. It was wonderful. I always knew I could count on her to be there for me, laugh with me, correct my spelling for me (or at least laugh at me because of it). She always took my side when I had an argument with my husband. Unless I was really off base, she told me. We even trained for a marathon together. Trisha and Nicole could conquer the world. I was sure of it.

On the day I started my conversation with God in the car, I was on my way to meet Nicole for a post-marathon run. I don't remember telling her that day, but I can't imagine that I wouldn't. I told her everything—the good, the bad, and the ugly. Unfortunately, I believe, she was whom I offended the most with my new freedom. At first she said, "Good for you, Trisha. That's great for *you*."

Shortly after that started the eye rolling, and she would say "Okay, Trisha, enough already."

Then: "I believe in God and everything, but my faith is private. Why do you keep talking and asking me about it?" Then finally she said, "All you ever want to do is save me. I can't even talk to you."

I was brokenhearted.

The one person besides my family, whom I cared the most about, didn't want to be my plus one anymore. She didn't like the transformation that had occurred. I wanted so badly for her to experience what I had found in Christ. I wanted her to understand that I *couldn't* think or do anything else. I couldn't take no for an answer. I was the opposite of happy.

During this same time, we were losing everything that had a dollar sign attached to it. House, gone. Cars, hauled off on flatbeds. Toys, returned to the dealers. Bank account, bankrupt. Up until that point, we had been doing pretty well at keeping up with the Joneses. We had fooled everyone, including ourselves, that we were happy in our lives. Maybe that's the point. Maybe we were "happy" by the world's standards; we had all the things, but we didn't have the unwavering joy of the Lord. Joy doesn't change when you lose your house or file for bankruptcy with your eleven-day-old son puking in his car seat in the middle of court proceedings. Joy doesn't leave when you find yourself packing up your beautiful two-story home in front of all the neighborhood to see. Joy is still left.

The joy of the Lord is my strength.

I had thought Nicole was my strength. If I had her support, then I would be okay. No wonder God separated us. We were terrible for each other. I was terrible for her. Her marriage didn't withstand it. I'm not at all saying I caused her divorce, but I certainly didn't help it. If I was more important to her than her husband, how could that be good? If I had put myself in the position for her to so extremely need me, how would that help her marriage or *her* at all, for that matter? No one should have to bear that weight. No one is meant to bear that weight but Jesus. Jesus says, "Come to me, all who labor and are heavy laden, and I will give you rest. Take my yoke upon you, and learn from me, for I am gentle and lowly in heart, and you will find rest for your souls. For my yoke is easy, and my burden is light" (Matthew 11:28–30).

We are not meant to bear all the weight of others. "We are to humble ourselves before the Lord and cast all our cares on Him because He cares for us. Then be sober-minded and watchful to resist the devil because he is like a roaring lion seeking someone to devour" (1 Peter 5:6–8).

I needed to humble myself before the Lord. I wasn't and am not anyone's savior. I need to think clearly and carry the yoke *with* Jesus. Then the enemy will have no place here. Jesus is free to delight in me, and I will continue to have joy whether in good circumstances or bad.

We have talked a lot about Moses (and me) so far. Now let's take a break from that and talk about a man named Paul for a minute.

Paul had a wild testimony. Here's a little back story on him. He was a Pharisee. That was his job. There were two groups of religious leaders at the time, the Pharisees and the Sadducees. You could think of them almost like politicians. You wouldn't know what they believed by looking at them, and most Pharisees or Sadducees didn't get paid for being one, just like a Democrat or Republican. Most people don't get paid for being a Democrat, but some do.

There are some huge differences between the two groups. One big difference was that the Sadducees didn't believe in heaven. They were "sad, you see." That's a good way to remember that difference.

There are also a lot of similarities between these religious leaders; they both wanted to uphold God's laws. They wanted so badly to uphold God's laws that they made hundreds of laws to ensure that God's laws weren't broken. For example, if God had a law that said you couldn't touch a Starbucks coffee cup, then the religious leaders thought, *Well, we should make a law saying people cannot touch the table the cup is sitting on.* And then they made another law stating that you cannot stand on the rug under the table that the cup is sitting on.

Then another law stated that you couldn't enter the *room* where the rug was in, that the table was on, where the forbidden cup sat.

Their intention was to follow God, but they got twisted and ended up focusing so much on the laws *they* had made that they never thought about God's law. Then they demanded obedience to *their* laws from God's people.

God was offering freedom, but the Pharisees and Sadducees spoke only of law, no grace.

I think of God's law like this. In our house when the kids were small, we didn't have a fence in the yard. So every time we went outside, I had to chase them all around to make sure they didn't run out into the road and get seriously hurt. The kids couldn't see or understand the danger that was right there, only steps away. But as their parent, I could see and know the street was dangerous and that they needed to be protected from it. Not only that, but once we got a fence, the kids were free to run around the yard, play on the playset, and slide down the slide without me chasing them, grabbing them, and yelling at them to stay out of the street. They were free inside the fence.

This is what God's law is, a protection and also a *great* freedom. God's people are able to run free inside His beautiful fence. The Pharisees and other religious leaders were creating a prison, not freedom.

Back to Paul. He was traveling "for work" down a dirt road

to the city of Damascus. As a Pharisee, his job was to find and kill all followers of "The Way" (aka Christians). So again, he was heading down the street, minding his own business, and plotting to kill all Christians in the town of Damascus when bam! A bolt of lightning flashed all around him. Then he heard a voice saying, "Saul, Saul, why are you persecuting Me?"

So Paul asked, "Who are You, Lord?" (By the way, if you hear a voice, it's always good to ask who it is who is talking to you.)

And He said, "I am Jesus, whom you are persecuting."

Paul had a lightning strike of a conversion. He was walking down the road to kill Christians, and his mission was changed in an instant. He was on the *right* road; he just had the *wrong* mission.

That was the same with me on the day I was converted. I was on a road of running for my own glory, to be the person others envied and were jealous of, when lightning struck and my mission completely changed. I was on the right road but wrong mission. My mission changed to run for God's glory and be the person others are drawn to Christ through.

Paul went on to be one of the greatest Bible teachers ever recorded. He wrote most of the New Testament to teach and encourage the first-century church. His letters still teach us today. Some of us need more of a lightning strike than a nudge.

After Paul had years of ministry work, God told him to go to Rome. Thankfully he was imprisoned and hitched a ride to Rome. That's not the transportation I would want, but it was a gift nonetheless. He was off to Rome. During his journey they ran into a great storm that left them shipwrecked. This guy had quite the journey. Wouldn't you have been frustrated?

What is going on, Lord? You told me to go to Rome. I didn't really think that would mean I would be put in prison and be hauled to Rome for a trial … I was thinking more like a first-class, direct flight. But now here I am shipwrecked in the middle of the ocean. Did I hear You wrong? Am I going to Rome?

Then Gods was like, "Listen. You don't have any money. I

got you transportation to Rome. Also, I'm not ready for you to get there just yet, so take a little break, a vacation on this beautiful beach." (Interpretation Of Trisha "the IOT."–my own, made up bible translation)

During said vacation, Paul sat around the fire with the local villagers. I imagine them telling stories or playing charades because they didn't speak the same language. Whatever they were doing, they were interrupted when a viper leaped out of the fire and latched onto Paul's arm (that part is true). When Paul had gathered a bundle of sticks and put them on the fire, a viper came out because of the heat and fastened on his hand. Look at the natives' response to the circumstances. "They said to one another 'no doubt this man is a murderer. Though he escaped from the sea, Justice has not allowed him to live'" (Acts 28:3–4).

The natives saw the viper on Paul's hand and decided "karma" was getting even with this man. It (karma or justice) would kill him, because *obviously* he must be a murderer if this was happening to him.

Paul's response was this: "He, however, shook off the creature into the fire and suffered not harm" (Acts 28:5).

Paul looked at his hand (his circumstance) and said, "Well, this can't be the end because God told me I am going to Rome." When he reminded himself of the truth God had told him, he was able to look at this threat and say, "Nope, not today. I will shake you right into the fire because God says this isn't how it ends for me. I'm going to Rome."

The native villagers watched this whole thing and then "waited for him to swell up or suddenly fall down dead" (Acts 28:6). They knew the circumstances said Paul was going to die. They knew … until they didn't. "But when they had waited a long time and saw no misfortune come to him, they changed their minds and said he was a god (Acts 28:6).

Their beliefs swung all the way from "You're a murderer and deserve to die and you will die" to "You must be a god." The villagers in this story let what was happening around them decide what to believe. They could change whom they believed in and what they believed in one evening around a fire.

Paul, on the other hand, was as cool as a cucumber. He could see what was happening all around him. His God was leading him, and he needed only to believe and follow. Joy lived here.

Anyone catch that it was a snake that jumped out of the fire to distract and tempt Paul into doubting the promises and goodness of God? That slimy cockroach showed up everywhere. When we hang onto the word of God and the truth of His promises, we can shake that snake off and continue on with our mission. Joy lives here.

During this time of feeling abandoned by *my person*, losing all the material possessions we had worked our whole lives for, and knowing life as we knew it was forever changed, joy lived there.

The joy of the Lord won't be shaken or moved. Happiness is fleeting and unstable. Joy is never changing. Nothing can come against my joy—not a loss of a job, child, home, car, or even one's very best friend. Sadness will come, but the joy of the Lord remains.

Thank You, Lord, for the blessing of joy. Shame, you have no place here. My joy is in the Lord. What next?

CHAPTER 12

Be Still

For God is not a God of disorder, but of peace.
—1 Corinthians 14:33

No discipline seems pleasant at the time, but painful.
Later on, however, it produces a harvest of righteousness
and peace for those who have been trained by it.
—Hebrews 12:11

I have been on a fad diet most of my life, or so it seems. Every time I got my hopes up that this diet was going to be the one to *finally* make me skinny fast, I worked the program perfectly for a few days, sometimes weeks, but I never reached the "skinny" goal. Yes, at times I lost a lot of weight but never felt as if I had arrived at my mysterious goal weight. Actually, I have never hit the 130-pound goal I set for myself. (Did I just tell you all that I have always in my adult life weighed more than 130 pounds? Yes, I did. I hope that helps you in some way. Ha.) Something tells me that even if I hit my magic scale number, it wouldn't feel successful. You tell me. I'm sure there is *someone* who has lived at 130 pounds her whole life, right? Is your life perfect? Or is 120 pounds where perfection comes? Or 115?

Saying it like that puts things into perspective for me. How could I place perfection on a number on an electronic scale?

Why do I ask that thing, the scale, every morning whether I am successful? Why does my day's peace depend on whether the electronic device can tell me, "Today you can have peace" or "Oops. Today is anxiety for you"? As a result, I think (unconsciously or consciously), *Today is going to be bad.* So, of course, my husband is terrible. My kids are disobedient that day. Work is totally unsatisfying. I don't even think my friends *like* hanging out with me. This is what is going on in my head. Is any of this true?

How come on days when the scale says, "Yeah, you lost two pounds today!" my day is great? On those days, the kids can spill red nail polish on the white rug, and I will run to their rescue and love them and teach them that everyone makes mistakes and messes up sometimes. "I'm so glad it was just polish and not gasoline!" Okay, maybe I'm exaggerating, but you get the point.

What if the beauty is in the order and discipline and not in the promised land? To me the promised land was 130 pounds. What happens if I never step foot on that land? What if I have to watch people walking all around me in the promised land I have created and never get to go there? What then?

I wasn't planning to have this book be all about Moses, but apparently that's where it is. Can you see where I'm going? Let's catch up with him. We know already God set Moses up to have a very clear path. Maybe it wasn't straight in Moses's mind, but God had it laid out in front of him anyway. Do you ever feel like God is trying to direct you to someplace or somewhere, but it doesn't seem to make any sense? Until it does. That is where we left Moses. His brother was now going to speak for him to the king, and eventually God's people would be set free. So they went to the palace (miracle one, miracle two, plague one, plague two). What if they would have said, "This is getting really tough. I think we should just quit" or "Pharaoh is never going to let our people go. What on earth is God having me do?" and just walked away? Maybe they did walk away a few times, possibly many times, but we know from scripture that by the tenth plague, Pharaoh gave in. God guided Moses every step of the way. Was there confusion all around? Yes, but not by God or even Moses. He knew by now that God was in control and had a plan. The world can be, and is most of the time, in a state of confusion and chaos, but God is a God not of disorder but of peace. Moses could peacefully walk into the palace, make his demands, and watch it all unfold. He didn't need to be short with the guard when he walked in or mad at the hardening of Pharaoh's heart. He was at peace.

I don't have to look at the chaos of this world. I no longer needed to focus on my parents while I was under the counter. The chaos disappeared, and I was left with Jesus. You don't have to be confused by the commotion in *your* life. You have a Peacemaker right by your side, ready for you to walk in peace *through* the chaos. He didn't take the chaos away from Moses. It was still all going on around him. Pharaoh was still rejecting his commands. Moses wasn't getting the job done in the Israelites' mind. He was failing miserably to all the people around him.

Maybe the Israelites thought Moses was a success based on what happened next before they left Egypt. The final plague came, and Pharaoh said, "Fine. Get out of here. I can't take it any longer."

Exodus 12:35–36 says, "The people of Israel had done as Moses had told them, for they had asked the Egyptians for silver and gold jewelry and for clothing and the Lord had given the people favor in the sight of the Egyptians, so that they let them have what they asked. Thus they plundered the Egyptians."

So if I lost you there, let me explain. God knew He was bringing His people to their promised land. Well, they couldn't go there without any money to build their homes or clothes to wear and so forth. So he told the housewives to go door to door and ask for all the Egyptians' stuff, and the Egyptians said, "Okay! Here you go. Have *all* our things. You want silver? Let me open the safe. You need gold? Are fifty bars okay? Here you go." Do you think there was chaos in the world when the Israelites left the city? Absolutely. Pharaoh actually said (14:5), "What is this that we have done, that we have let Israel go from serving us?" But were God and His people still in order? Yep, they had what they needed and were off to the promised land.

We already know the people were quite upset when they found themselves stuck between an army and an ocean but not God. Here's a great reminder what God's response was to the situation. Moses said, "Fear not, stand firm, and see the salvation of the Lord, which he will work for you today. For the Egyptians who you see today, you shall never see again. The Lord will fight for you, and you have only to be silent" (14:13–14).

Is being silent hard for anyone else? One day I looked around my house and saw these verses all over. Apparently every time I went to Hobby Lobby, I bought a sign that said, "Be Still and Know" or "The Lord will fight for you if you are only still or silent." Huh, was the Lord trying to tell me something? *Rest in Me*, He whispers. Sometimes he needs to shout this if I find myself getting entangled in the chaos of life rather than resting in the peace of God or the discipline of walking hand and hand with my Creator. It's the rest, the quiet discipline of order in the day to day, that gives me peace, that lets me sit back and watch the world swirl around me, and I'm not tempted to get caught up in the tornado. I can be still and know He is God and that *I* am not. I am able to wait on Him to do God stuff. No one wants to see Trisha stuff when we can watch God stuff.

God says, "Sit back … be still. I will fight. I will part the seas. I will work on your spouse. I will call your children to me. I will battle the cancer. I will deal with the mother-in-law. I will write this book. You be still."

It is almost like I hear God whisper to me, "Soak it all in, in the peace of the sidelines until I call you into the game. *Until* I tell you to *go*! Then and only then can you walk on dry ground, pockets full, and hearts at peace. You cannot go until you first are still!"

CHAPTER 13

Heavy Praise

The Lord is my strength and my song;
He has given me victory.
This is my God, and I will praise him—
My father's God, and I will exalt him!
—Exodus 15:2

What do we do when we cannot lift our arms to praise? Where do I go from there? How do I get out of bed when the weight of my circumstances is so heavy? How can I continue when I am just *so* tired? Even just in the mundaneness (I'm not sure whether that is a word) of life?

Being a parent is sometimes like Chinese water torture[12]. One small drip at a time in the same place over and over and over and over *and* over again. Each drip itself is nothing. No one would think anything of one drop of rain on his or her forehead. No one would think it would be hard to deal with doing one load of laundry, cleaning one plate, picking up one dirty sock, or resolving one fight or … You fill in the blank. But when life is dish after dish, load after load, fight after fight, one hard thing after another and another and another, the process can be torture. Torture no

---

[12] (I have no idea if this is actually the way to torture someone in China, but you know what I mean)

107

one can see or measure or even *know* about sometimes. But God knows.

After Moses and the Israelites crossed the sea onto dry land and made it to the other side, they praised God. Moses stopped and even wrote God a song, expressing how much he praised Him and how much he was in awe of God. They all sang it together.

> I will sing to the Lord, for he has triumphed gloriously;
> The horse and his rider he has thrown into the sea.
> The Lord is my strength and my song, and he has become my salvation;
> This is my God and I will praise him, my father's God, and I will exalt him.
> The Lord is a man of war; the Lord is his name.
> Pharaoh's chariots and his host he cast into the sea, and his chosen officers were sunk in the Red Sea.
> The floods covered them; they went down into the depths like a stone.
> Your right hand, O Lord, glorious in power, your right hand, O Lord shatters the enemy.
> In the greatness of your majesty you overthrow your adversaries; you send out your fury; it consumes them like stubble.
> At the blast of your nostrils the waters piled up; the floods stood up in a heap; the deep congealed in the heart of the sea.
> The enemy said, "I will pursue, I will overtake, I will divide the spoil; my desire shall have its fill of them.

I will draw my sword; my hand shall destroy
them."

You blew with your wind; the sea covered
them; they sank like lead in the mighty waters.

Who is like you, O Lord, among the gods?

Who is like you, majestic in holiness, awesome
in glorious deeds, doing wonders?

You stretched out your hand; the earth
swallowed them.

–Exodus 15:1-10

Moses was so extremely grateful for who God is and what
He had done for them. The moment God saw His people had
followed Him onto the dry ground, He lowered their enemy in
there with them. It seems strange, doesn't it? Why wouldn't God
just block the waters so the enemy couldn't step foot on the dry
ground? They could just stand on the shore and watch as the
people walked free and would be able to do nothing about it …
Today at least.

God wouldn't leave them to be a future threat. He drew the
chariots and soldiers, the very people who had denied Him over
and over. The same people who had chance after chance to *see*
what and *who* God is, and they still denied Him. They turned
their backs on truth and followed the ways of their gods. They
went their own way. They followed what seemed right in their
heart.

Jeremiah 17:9 says, "The heart [is] deceitful above all [things],
and desperately wicked."

The enemy of God's people was God's to deal with. The people
just needed to keep their eyes on God, their Savior, Redeemer,
Lord—their audience of One. So their enemy wasn't just being
stopped; he was being obliterated, never to be a threat to them
again in that way. They were free. They were winning. So they
continued to praise Him.

"You have led in your steadfast love the people whom you have redeemed; You have guided them by your strength to your holy abode. The peoples have heard; they tremble" (Exodus 15:13–15).

They continued to sing to the Lord for His goodness, strength, and mercy. They ended with the following: "The Lord will reign forever and ever" (Exodus 15:18).

If we ended right here, this would be a great ending. Moses had a rough start; he went from the river to the palace and then to the wilderness as the deliverer, and God was with him every step of the way. So in the end they praised. The end. What a perfect ending.

I love romantic comedies or, even more, Hallmark movies. My husband and son hate them. Our son, Cash, says, "They are so annoying. First they accidentally meet, hate each other,. Then they start to like each other, get into a fight, make up and kiss … the end." Okay, so he might have a point. But I think the reason I like them so much is because we get to see the falling-in-love part, the butterflies and unknowns. Then the story ends before life gets real. I have enough "real life" that I enjoy watching the beauty of the beginning before it's all messy and complicated. Yes, the beginning can be messy and complicated, but it is also filled with so much hope for a happy ending.

The Israelites didn't continue their attitude of praise. They got thirsty and hungry.

Ever heard of "hangry"? "Han-gry /Han-gree/adj: an anger fueled by hunger or google dictionary says—"bad-tempered or irritable as a result of hunger." A cranky state resulting from lack of food, especially sweet things."

That is what happened to the people of God. They were *hangry*. We weren't surprised that God had provided for them because we know the story. We have read the story. God made the bitter water sweet. He made bread and meat fall from the sky. Moses struck a rock, and the Lord made water so they could live. (We will talk more about these things in the next chapters.) But what about your life? Are you surprised when God shows up? Shocked that He knows what is going on? I can lean towards this more often than not.

It turns out they weren't alone in the wilderness. There were other nations fighting for this piece of sand and rock. "So Moses said to Joshua [commander and leader of their army], 'Choose for us men, and go out and fight with Amalek. Tomorrow I will stand on the top of the hill with the staff of God in my hand'" (Exodus 17:9–10).

They were going to war, and Moses got a plan from the Lord. "Get some guys together to fight, and I will watch with my brother, Aaron, and my buddy Hur, with God's staff. Sounds good, right?" And Joshua did as Moses said. "Whenever Moses held up his hand, Israel prevailed, and whenever he lowered his hand, Amalek prevailed" (Exodus 17:11)

Moses figured out the formula for victory. Lift your hands to the Lord! Don't lift your hands to the Lord …fail. Do you see what we need to learn here? Lift your hands to the Lord. Praise God in all circumstances.

Have you ever been in an amazing worship setting? Maybe a concert or just an awesome Sunday morning or Tuesday afternoon in your kitchen. After a while of holding your hands high to the Lord, they start to get tired. Mine probably get tired faster than yours, but that's what happens when you aren't all the way in shape (smiley face). Well, this same thing happened to Moses. "But Moses' hands grew weary, so they took a stone and put it under him, and he sat on it, while Aaron and Hur held up his hands, one on one side, and the other on the other side. So his hands were steady until the going down of the sun" (Exodus 17:12).

I had to take a pause for a minute after reading this. His *people* came and held up his arms in praise. His *people* sat him down and said, "It's okay that you can't do it right now. We will do it for you." Moses wasn't alone. He didn't have to physically lift himself up to be victorious. He just had to get himself to a place where he was surrounded by people who would lift him up in times of trouble. They would lift him up when he was too weak to just praise. I believe this same thing is true both spiritually and physically. Have you been there? Too weak to even praise God? Too weighed down by the challenges of this life? Too exhausted by trying again and again and still not succeeding? I know I have time and time again. But we can't stop there. We need to look around and see whether we already put ourselves in a place with at least *a* person on each side, *a* person willing to lift our arms when we cannot.

I told you I had to ask someone to be my friend when I first became a Christian. I knew even then that I would need someone to help when times became hard. I knew I couldn't walk this life out alone. I took the first step. I took the first leap of faith to start a community around me. If you don't have people (or a person), ask others to be your people. Make the first step. If a community already surrounds you, use it to hold you up. Ask for prayer. Be vulnerable with trusted friends who love the Lord.

Let me tell you about *my* people. God has been so faithful. In almost a decade, God has filled my life with some amazing people. I don't see them all every day, but each one has helped, encouraged, challenged, inspired, and held me up in times when I couldn't lift my hands to the Lord. Without these people in my life, my walk with the Lord would have looked much different— more distant and on a surface level. I would have sugarcoated things and not worked so hard to do hard things, like write a book, love my husband, or take my health seriously. Or even challenge myself to teach Bible study to our kids. I needed my people to lift my hands in praise when I couldn't see anything to praise about. Their names may not be Aaron or Hur, but I have been victorious because of their strength. And I pray I have done (even half) the same for them.

Heavy praise isn't easy. It isn't for the faint of heart. This is hard work, but again God is so faithful and true. He will never leave you or forsake you. He will be there to help you praise as well. How mind blowing is that. The God of the universe not only wants praise but helps you praise Him. Roman 8:26 says, "Likewise the Spirit helps us in our weakness. For we do not even know what to pray for as we ought, but the Spirit himself intercedes for us with groaning too deep for words."

The words "the Spirit himself" get me every time. He Himself intercedes or prays for me. What? Here's another one, just a couple of verses before this one. "The Spirit Himself testifies with our spirit that we are children of God" (Romans 8:16).

When or if we don't feel like children of God, the Spirit testifies to our spirit that we *are* children of God. He testifies for us, lifting up our hands to praise Him.

This is my prayer for us: "Now may the Lord of peace Himself continually grant you peace in every circumstance. The Lord be with you all!" (2 Thessalonians 3:16).

CHAPTER 14

Sweet Wine

And in that day the mountains shall drip sweet wine,
and the hills shall flow with milk,
and all the stream beds of Judah shall flow with water;
and a fountain shall come forth from the house
of the Lord and water the valley of Shittim.

—Joel 3:18

Have you ever been to a wedding? I *love* weddings. Of course I do. A wedding is like a living and breathing Hallmark movie, with all the love and squishy feelings in the air. In my mind as a woman, everyone is so happy to be dressed up and catching up with old friends and family she hasn't seen in months or even sometimes years. The laughter is booming at the reception party after the ceremony. Our shoes go flying off at the first sound of the first fast song I can dance with my girls, and I snuggle with my husband on the slow ones. Awww, I love weddings.

Jesus even attended a wedding. Everyone was there, including His mother, friends, and disciples. Like most weddings, there was a snag, but this was no small one. They ran out of wine!

In an article called "A crisis of wine and joy in Cana" says– "The social contract: remember, this is the Middle East. That means the host has certain social obligations regarding his clan and the community (often one and the same) concerning this marriage feast, one of which is reciprocal hospitality. For example, if last year I invited you to my son's marriage feast, fed you lavishly, and provided you with all the wine you cared to drink, it is a given that you will (and must) do the same for me when I attend your son's marriage feast. Failure to respond in kind comes with severe social consequences.

- The marriage would forever be branded a disgrace, the host family would be shamed, and the newly married couple would carry a social stigma of shame with them for the rest of their days, as would their children and their children's children.
- Who would ever want to arrange a marriage with any of his or her offspring, the legacy of such a disastrous marriage feast? Whatever joy was being toasted, experienced, and celebrated during the feast up to this point would be immediately transformed to anger, scorn, and derision.
- Some commentators suggest that those other families who had previously hosted this family at their respective marriage feasts would have had grounds for a lawsuit for damages if they weren't treated in kind. That's how severe a breach of the reciprocal hospitality code this would have been.
- Any steward associated with such a marriage feast disaster would never work another wedding in that community again."[13]

No small snag.

"When the wine ran out, the Mother of Jesus said to him, 'They have not wine.' And Jesus said to her, 'Woman, what does that have to do with me? My hour has not yet come'" (John 2:3).

---

[13] Preserving Bible Times Inc. "A crisis of wine and joy in Cana"
(6.The NET Bible, First Edition [Biblical Studies Press, 2005], p. 2024 footnote.)

First of all, "woman" was a sign of respect back then. Jesus used it a couple of more times to address His mother. This wasn't disrespectful like it would sound now if my son said it to me. Yikes! A few days ago I had my forty-first birthday. I was up for a few hours, and my daughters ran up to me and gave me hugs and birthday wishes. My husband wished me happy birthday before he left for work, but my son never said anything. He hugged me like normal. He made his breakfast and started his school work like normal but never acknowledged my birthday.

Huh? I thought. So I said, "Hey, bud, did you know it's my birthday?"

He looked up for his book and said in a very monotone, "Oh, happy birthday." I of course was hurt by this, and when he saw I was hurt, he said rudely "What? You probably don't want people to acknowledge your birthday anymore because you are so old."

That was rude! On the other hand, what Jesus did to His mother by calling her "woman" was respectful. By the way, my boy is normally very sweet, but this was a man-foot-in-mouth moment he better have learned from and *will not* repeat.

Jesus's mother must have known Jesus was going to do something because she said to the servants, "Do whatever he tells you" (John 2:5) "Now there were six stone water jars there for the Jewish rites of purification, each holding twenty or thirty gallons. Jesus said to the servants, 'Fill the jars with water.' And they filled them up to the brim" (John 2:7).

These jars were normally used for cleaning dirt and grime off the Jewish peoples' hands before they entered a holy place. The six jars together probably held between 120 and 180 gallons of water. That was a lot of water for washing, but it certainly wasn't meant for drinking water. So the servants were probably surprised when Jesus told them to "draw some out and take it to the master of the feast" (John 2:8).

Has God ever asked you to do something that was kind of weird? I have. I once heard a story about a worship leader who during a Sunday morning set suddenly stopped playing the piano, crawled under the piano, and started barking like a dog. Weird? Yes, but as the story is told, what happened next was amazing. A man stood up in the middle of the congregation with tears streaming down his face, walked up front, and gave his life to Christ. Apparently he had been having a conversation with God and said, "God, if You are real, make that man crawl under the piano and bark like a dog." So when he saw this crazy, weird act of the worship leader, he had to give his life over immediately. Wow, if that story is real, what faith the worship pastor had to follow through with that call.

I am really glad I haven't had to crawl under a piano and bark like a dog. My friends and I even have a saying to try to make us feel better about doing "strange things" God sometimes calls us to do. We say, almost like an exciting declaration of what's to come, "Let's get weird." Maybe it feels better because we aren't alone in the "weird."

I imagine the servants looking at one another, shrugging, and then saying, "Let's get weird." The master of the feast was the guest of honor, so if they offended him, it would be curtains for the host. This was a huge risk. *But* "let's get weird." So they did as Jesus asked and filled the pitchers all the way to the top with water from the purification jars. Then they took the pitchers to the master of the feast. And like Jesus had told them, they poured the water into the man's glass.

They must have been terrified, thinking, *What on earth is this guy having me do? What is the guest of honor going to do to me when he sees I have poured old, dirty water into his wine glass? This is going to disgrace him so badly. Why would Jesus tell me to do this? Is he playing a mean joke or what?*

At this point in Jesus's life, He hadn't performed any miracles yet. He hadn't *outed* Himself as being the Savior of the world or Son of God Almighty. He was at this point just a guy, a really good guy, since He had never sinned. That fact must have been noticed to some degree. He never dishonored His parents, never told a little white lie, never cheated in cards, never cheated on His taxes or stole from His neighbor. Never. At this point He was just a great guy. Isaiah even said He wasn't a good-looking guy. He was just average, not someone you would take a second look at as He was walking down the street or appearing at a wedding.

"He had no form or majesty that we should look at him, and no beauty that we should desire him" (Isaiah 53:2). This verse still surprises me. I have always thought of Jesus as beautiful, with dark hair and skin and piercing blue eyes that drew you in with just one look. But this description doesn't even make sense. What Middle Eastern person do you know with blue eyes? I guess I had just decided in my mind that He looked like that, but He didn't. He was average, maybe even unattractive.

Pretend you are a servant at the wedding. This average, no-name guy tells you to pour water into wine glasses at a fancy wedding. What do you do? How do you feel?

The servants did it anyway.

Then and only *after* they poured out the water, made the act of faith, and stepped into the unknown, scary place of pure obedience (watching and waiting while the master picked up the water and tipped the glass to drink), the miracle happened. "When the master of the feast tasted the water now become wine" (John 2:9).

Talk about waiting until the last minute to show yourself God. Jesus waited until the water reached the master's lips to turn it into wine—and not just any cheap wine; it was the good stuff. "When the master of the feast tasted the water now become wine, and did not know where it came from (though the servants who had drawn the water knew), the master of the feast called the bridegroom and said to him, 'Everyone serves the good wine first, and when people have drunk freely, then the poor wine. But you have kept the good wine until now.'"

Isn't that the truth of all of us? We give our best self first. And what's left over is us. When Nate and I were dating, I liked all sorts of things he liked. I liked watching prospecting shows with him and hockey games. First of all, prospecting? Who likes watching that? Watching someone pan for gold on TV? Maybe if I was there in the mountains and kneeling down in the river, finding my own treasures, I would like that, but not watching someone else do it on TV. But I watched it with him because I wanted him to like me. I put my best flexible self forward.

He did the same. He would go to romantic comedies with me at the theater. He even (after dating for only a few months) got into a minivan with my mom, my brother and his wife, and their eighteen-month-old baby. We drove to Colorado for a wedding. I found out later that small spaces and a lot of people weren't his first choice. But he put his best self first.

Not God. He breaks out the great wine at the *end* of the party. I love it. The best is yet to come. "This, the first of his signs, Jesus did in Cana in Galilee, and manifested his glory. And his disciples believed in him" (John 2:11).

This was just Jesus's first sign, the tip of the iceberg. It really was His great press release. This was the first time He showed Himself to be God. This was the very first time anyone saw Him do a miracle. If you study the Gospels, you will see that every time Jesus did a miracle, it was so people would believe.

John said at the end of the Gospel book, "Now Jesus did many other signs in the presence of the disciples, which are not written in this book; but these are written so that you may believe that Jesus is the Christ, the Son of God, and that by believing you may have life in his name" (John 20:30–31).

So Jesus picked this sign, turning water into wine, to be his debut miracle. This was to tell the world that He was the Christ or at the very least to get the ball rolling. Whom did He debut for? Who even knew about the wonder? Who knew the glass had been filled with water first?

Jesus, *maybe* His mom, and the servants.

Think about the last wedding you went to. What was your server's name? What did he or she look like? Can you remember?

I can't. Servants are behind the scenes at weddings. Everyone is busy catching up with old friends and family, laughing, and dancing. The servants are unseen. And the servants are whom Jesus decided to show Himself to first?

Have you ever felt unseen?

I know I have. When I first heard this story and saw what Jesus did with the servants, I felt completely blessed. I am walking through a season where I can tend to *feel* unseen by my family. The mundaneness of my daily duties can easily get overlooked. What my days are filled with doesn't seem earth shattering or altogether too important by itself. So the big "attaboy" obviously doesn't come at the end of each day.

I was feeling rather down about this recently, really feeling like I *deserved* credit. I was getting sick of being overlooked. Basically I had a really bad attitude. It got me thinking about the servants. What do you think their response was after seeing this miracle? Do you think they shouted, "Hey, everyone I poured the glass" or "The guy over there, the average-looking guy—he just turned the water into wine, *but* I poured it into the glass. Look at *my* skills"? Is that how you imagine them responding? Me neither. I imagine them being stunned to silence, to be so awe inspired as to know and follow this man. They wanted to get as close to Him as they possibly could and not leave His side. I imagine after the shock and awe wore off enough to get their words back, they whispered into each other's ears, "It was Jesus. He is the Christ." They never thought about themselves once. It was all about Christ Jesus. They were so thankful to be near Him—to smell His skin, touch His face, and look into His dark-brown eyes. They weren't looking for praise; they were praising the One worthy of praise.

The servants differed drastically from whom we have been looking at, the Israelites. But they also were witnessing water changing. Look at this.

After they left the Red Sea, they walked for three days and found no water. "When they came to Marah, they could not drink the water of Marah because it was bitter; therefore it was named Marah. And the people grumbled against Moses, saying, 'What shall we drink?'" (Exodus 15:23–24).

I'm sure the people at the wedding would have been saying the same thing if they would have caught wind that the wine was out. "So Moses cried to the Lord, and the Lord showed him a log, and he threw it into the water, and the water became sweet" (Exodus 15:25).

The Israelites grumbled to a man, but Moses cried out to the Lord. Which one helped? Man, I do like to complain sometimes, but it never makes me feel better and *never* solves the problem. I want to be like the servants at the wedding, who were blindly obedient and awestruck. Not the grumbling Israelites, although they didn't drink anything for three days. Yikes. I need to not be too hard on them.

Nate and I both serve in our church youth group. One week before I went in, I decided this would be a great time to tell Nate this revelation I had had with the Lord. "I don't need praise or recognition, I need to praise and recognize the Miracle Maker!"

The church was booming with the hustle and bustle of hundreds of people all around: parents checking in their kids, kids high-fiving each other after a long couple of days of not seeing one another, and Nate and I standing in the middle of the room.

I am telling him basically this entire chapter. I don't know why he doesn't listen to me. Sometimes I pick such great places to tell him meaningful and life-changing stories and confessions. And that is what I was doing that night. I was confessing to Nate that I had been having a bad attitude and wanted his forgiveness. I told him I wanted to be more like the servants, who found that just being close to Jesus was the prize, not the praise of men. That there was reward in the smell of His word in the morning, looking at His face in the pages, or seeing His smile in my kids. I just want Jesus, not praise.

As I finished, we went into the service for the youth. We have an amazing youth band! Service started like any other night, first with amazing worship and then the message. This week our youth leader had a young lady give her testimony. This was rare, so I was really excited. I love testimonies. A girl named Emma went to the stage. She was on the worship team with our daughter, Elliot, but I'd had very little time to get to know her.

Emma went to the mic, and the first thing she said was. "Last year I went to a girls' youth camp. *Trisha* was speaking [yes, that's me, Trisha]." She continued to say, "The words she said really impacted me *and* still are. I am a different person since then. I now have a personal relationship with the Lord, and it has changed me, and I am so happy."

What? (Insert ugly cry.) *I had just told You, Lord, that I wanted to be like the servants. I don't need the praise of man. I just want You!*

I heard His still, small voice say, "This *is* being close to Me. I want you to know that I love you. I am proud of you, I see you, and I want to encourage you and lift you up to Me!"

You are too much to take sometimes, Lord. I was overwhelmed with every emotion. I was so thankful that someone had been impacted for Jesus by something I said. I was in shock at how loved and close I was to God's presence in that dark gymnasium. I was overcome with joy in serving. And I was even scared that this feeling wouldn't last forever, all at the same time.

That was one of the greatest gifts I have ever received from the Lord: to know that someone knows Jesus, and I had a small part in it. *Wow! Thank You, Jesus!*

I want to tell you that after I spoke the message Emma had talked about, I literally ran out of the room, crying, because I thought the whole message was squashed. At first I felt pretty good while speaking, and just as I was going to move into the *really good stuff*, my girl Elliot's hand went up in the crowd. I thought, *Oh, my sweet girl has a beautiful insight into what I am talking about, and she obviously can't keep it to herself.* That's what I had thought was happening. Nope, that wasn't it. She *actually* said, "Mom, a group of us were supposed to go horseback riding in like five minutes."

Okay? So I ran out of the room and cried while the youngest girls in the group went horseback riding.

This was the message that had touched Emma, the one that didn't even get to the "good part."

Of course it was all how it was supposed to be. After the younger girls left, the older girls all broke down and needed us to do small group prayer with them. So the leaders and I wiped *my* tears, and we went to work. It was amazing. But left on my own, I would have thought it was ruined. It certainly didn't go how I had imagined it in my mind. It turned out to be so much better.

Years ago, Johnny Carson had an eight-year-old boy from West Virginia on his show because he had rescued two friends in a coal mine outside his hometown. It became apparent that the boy was a Christian, so Johnny asked him whether he went to Sunday school. When he answered yes, Johnny asked him what he had learned there.

"Last week," he replied, "our lesson was about when Jesus went to a wedding and turned water into wine."

The audience roared, but Johnny kept right on and asked, "What did you learn from that?"

The boy squirmed in his chair and thought, then lifted his face and said, "If you're going to have a wedding, make sure you invite Jesus!"

I agree with this little man, and I'll add this. If you are going to do *anything*, *make sure* you invite Jesus.

CHAPTER 15

Heavenly Bread

I am the bread of life.

—Jesus

Recently I changed my mind-set on food. As you already know, this has been a lifelong struggle for me. It is the place where I have found great comfort and joy. It has always been there for me. When I needed a sugar high, a pick-me-up, or a little hug, food was there. I loved it. But it didn't always love me back.

What ended up happening was that I would go through this cycle when I felt bad or sad. I would eat something sweet, then need something salty, then go back sweet and salty until I was sick. The only time I felt better was for the three seconds the food was in my mouth, and even then it was a guilty pleasure. So the cycle continued until I would decide to cut out all sugar and junk food. Well, that lasted only until my next emotional crisis, and I jumped right back on the sugar train. What I realized is that the challenge isn't all about removing the bad; it is more about adding the good, and the bad will have less room to live.

Instead of just adding food, let's add love. The greatest commandment is to love—love God and people.

Francis Chan says in his book *Crazy Love*, "Imagine going for a run while eating a box of Twinkies. Besides being self-defeating and side-ache-inducing, it would also be near impossible, you would have to stop running in order to eat Twinkies. In the same way, you have to stop loving and pursuing Christ in order to sin."

The Israelites had a cycle of their own. Let me recap where they had come so far. First, they became slaves in Egypt. Then God freed His people through Moses. God gave them Himself as a guide, a GPS throughout their journey in the form of a pillar of cloud and fire. He parted the Red Sea *and* destroyed their enemies. The Israelites and Moses praised God. Then they got thirsty. God provided clean, sweet water. Over and over the Israelites doubted God, grumbled and complained, and God provided for them. Their food was no different.

Originally when they left Egypt, it should have taken them two weeks to get to the promised land. But because of their distrust, complaints, unbelief, and disobedience, their two-week trip turned into forty years of wandering.

God wanted to take His people out of their surroundings for a few weeks, even a year, so He could introduce Himself to them. Remember, they had been enslaved for four hundred years. God wanted to show them who He really was and what He had for them. "And He said, 'If you will give earnest heed to the voice of the Lord your God, and do what is right in His sight, and give ear to His commandments, and keep all His statutes, I will put none of the diseases on you which I have put on the Egyptians; for I, the Lord, am your healer'" (Exodus 15:26).

The very first introduction He made was that *He* was their healer. Remember, they were in an if/then covenant. So God was telling them, "*If* you listen to Me, *then* you will not have any diseases that the Egyptians have." He was telling them, "*I* will make sure you are healthy and cared for, I, God, and I alone." "Then they came to Elim, where there were twelve springs of water and seventy palm trees, and they encamped there by the water" (Exodus 15:27).

One of my mind shifts is the importance of adding water. Water is so important for your physical and mental health. If we have the correct amount of water in a day, we can do just about anything. Add water! Adding more water to my diet has changed how I function. It has added life to my body.

I'm sure the people were feeling great being next to the twelve springs of water. I bet they thought they would never thirst again (more on that in the next chapter).

But they had to keep moving forward; the pillar of cloud moved so they had to follow God's leading. They went from the city to the sea and to the springs of water, and now they had entered the wilderness. The wilderness of Sin was its name.

That was the name of the place they went to, Sin. The wilderness of Sin … Man, isn't it a wilderness?

I know when I was living a life of sin, that would have been a great way of describing it—the wilderness. Wandering around and wondering whether I would ever land in my promised land. But God was still there! He was still there when my parents got divorced or the time my brother and I had to go to a foster home because our mom hadn't come home. Or the morning we woke up in first grade to find our car spray-painted with curse words. God was there. I didn't know it, but it doesn't change the fact that He was there with me.

God was with the Israelites, and they knew it, but they didn't trust Him to provide. They kept going through the same cycle. Slavery to crying out to God. God provided, and they finally praised God. A challenge came in front of them, and the cycle repeated. They desired slavery and cried out to God, God provided, and they finally praised God.

Obviously, our bankruptcy really shook our lives. But the effects didn't stop with the last court date. Something like a bankruptcy or divorce can last well into the next season or seasons of your life. One of the ways I know this is because both of those events still follow me in this season right now.

Every time we go to make an investment, we tend to replay the financial crisis all over again. "Lord, don't let us make the same mistake again." That's on a good day, or the other way I could go is to not have a budget and just spend whatever I want on whatever I want all the time. Then I cry out to God because I can't pay the mortgage. The cycle continues, and God provides—it might not look like what I thought He would do, but He provides a way to pay or a way out, and *then* I praise God.

What if we reversed the cycle? What if I started with praising God, and then He would still provide? And then I would go right back to praising God instead of being in slavery? Skip slavery altogether. Skip the desperate crying, grumbling, and doubting. Just praise, sometimes with heavy praise.

What if the Israelites started with praising God? They had Him right there all the time. Cloud by day and fire by night. They could see the presence of God leading and guiding their steps. Starting with praise, they did not.

After the grumbling and complaining, the Lord said to Moses, "Behold, I am about to rain bread from heaven for you and the people shall go out and gather a day's portion every day" (Exodus 16:4).

God says, "I am about to rain bread from heaven for you!"

Ever heard of the verse "Give us this day our daily bread?" Well, this is what happened out there in the wilderness. God provided the people with literally their daily bread. Every morning they had to go out and gather the flake- or seedlike substance called "manna," which means "What is it?" Isn't that funny? They went out in the morning and gathered the substance, then looked at it and said, "What is it?"

Well, I guess it was their daily bread because at the end of the day, if any was left, it would rot and grow maggots. Yuck! The Israelites literally had to depend on God every day to provide food, and it lasted only one day. So the next morning they had to depend on God again to survive.

As I am writing this morning, I am stressed about a new business venture for me and Nate. I need this reminder! Lord, I need my daily bread. I know You are the Provider, but today I need a fresh reminder.

Jesus has something to say about this. He's going to make it rain!

The disciples had been walking with Jesus for a while now. They have watched Him heal many people, feed five thousand men (not including women and children), and walk on water. I mean seriously, one of these acts was enough to give them faith for a lifetime, right?

Of course, after all these miracles, Jesus developed a following. But back in Jesus's time, there weren't likes and swipe rights. They actually had to *follow* Him. They had to get into a boat and chase Him down, following. "So let's get in the boat and chase Jesus down." Read Jesus's response when the crowd found Him. John 6:26–40 says, "Truly, truly, I say to you, you are seeking me, not because you saw signs, but because you eat your fill of the loaves. Do not labor for the food that perishes, but for the food that endures to eternal life, which the Son of Man will give you. For him God the Father has set his seal."

Jesus was saying to the crowd, "You just want another free meal. I'm not just here to give out a lunch buffet. I have so much more for you." Naturally the people asked how to get this *more* He was offering.

This got me thinking. Do I just want a free meal of peace and joy He gave me last week? Or do I want *Him*?

The crowd said to Jesus, "What must we do to be doing the works of God?"

This is what we so often ask. "What can I do better? How can I earn Your favor, Your love, Lord?"

Jesus answered them, "This is the work of God, that you believe in him whom he has sent." That is the work we are to do: believe. And belief can be work sometimes.

The crowd following Jesus kept asking questions. "So they said to Him, 'What do You do for a sign, so that we may see, and believe You? What work do You perform? Our fathers ate the manna in the wilderness; as it is written, "He gave them bread out of heaven to eat."'"

What they are asking for was more evidence. They wanted more signs, more miracles. They wanted "What is it?" when "Who is it?" was right in front of them. How many times do *I* do that? How many times do I ask for what God can give me instead of seeing and believing He is all I need?

"An intimate encounter with Jesus is the most transforming experience of human existence. To know him as he is, is to come home. To have his life, joy, love and presence cannot be compared. A true knowledge of Jesus is our greatest need and our greatest happiness. To be mistaken about him is the saddest mistake of all" (John Eldredge) [14]

Jesus said to them, "*I am the bread of life*; he who comes to Me will not hunger, and he who believes in Me will never thirst" (John 6:26–35 emphasis added).

Have you ever felt unseen or used? I have. Sometimes I think the title "Mom" comes with a stamp that says, "Unseen and Used." What time is dinner? Where is my laundry? Why don't we have milk?

I almost feel that from Jesus right here. He is begging them to see Him for who He is and not what He can do for them. In the book *Polished and Concealed*, Rhianna says, "Seek His face."

I love this visual. Seek Jesus's face, not what He can do for you but who He is. He is God. He is love. He is peace. He is life. He is provision. He is never surprised. He is mine.

Lord, thank You for You. Thank You for always being right there next to me, waiting for me to turn and look. You are never far away. Forgive me for using You for Your gifts and miracles and not seeking, chasing, and following You alone, Amen.

---

[14] Beautiful Outlaw: Experiencing the Playful, Disruptive, Extravagant Personality of Jesus Paperback – April 23, 2013

CHAPTER 16

The Rock

My hope is built on nothing less
Than Jesus Christ, my righteousness;
I dare not trust the sweetest frame,
But wholly lean on Jesus' name.

—Edward Mote

At thirty-three years old, I could barely read. I could read but not confidently. I wouldn't even read to the kids. Or when I did, I hated it. Even then, I felt like they were judging me for my reading skill level or lack thereof. But I needed to know who Jesus was. So, I read everything to do with this Jesus *all* the time. The kids were little, so I read before they got up. I read at nap time. I read when they went to bed. All. The. Time. I couldn't get enough. I was hungry and thirsty for truth.

We read in the last chapter that the people of Israel grew hungry, but they also got thirsty, so thirsty. "All the congregation of the people of Israel moved on from the wilderness of Sin" (Exodus 17:1).

Sin was where they left, and they were thirsty. Man, does that sound like my life. I was living a life of sin, and when I left it, I was thirsty. Thirsty to know the Lord.

The Israelites were literally dying of thirst, *and* they were mad. Mad at Moses. They grumbled and complained to him over and over to find them water. Again they wished for the very slavery they had been freed from. "Why did you bring us up out of Egypt?" (Exodus 17:3).

We are hard on the Israelites for their little faith in God. Yes, they had seen some amazing things. Plagues descended, waters parted, food fell from the sky, water turned from bitter to sweet; but now they were three days without water and were genuinely thirsty. I would be, and you would be. But they took their eyes off God and looked at their circumstances. They had heavy arms. They changed from an audience of One to water. That was all they could think of every day.

In the Gospel of John, a woman was also thirsty. "Jesus, wearied from His journey, was sitting beside the well. It was about the sixth hour. A woman from Samaria came to draw water" (John 4:4).

They talked for a little bit. Jesus asked her to draw Him some water. It is so hard to imagine Jesus as fully God and fully man. But here He was, fully man; He was weary from His journey and sat down, asking a *Samaritan woman* to fetch Him water. That interaction was a definite no-no to the Jewish customs. The Samaritans had been enemy number one for seven hundred years. They had walked away from the Jewish religion and stopped sacrificing at the temple along with doing many other offenses to the Jews. In fact, the woman called Him on it. "How is it that you, a Jew, ask for a drink from me, a woman of Samaria?" (John 4:9).

Jesus explained to her that He was the bearer of living water, that this water in the cistern was still water, and that she would become thirsty again after she drank it. Jesus was offering her living water—rushing, living, moving, breathing water. It was water that gave life.

Hold that story for just a minute. Let's go back to Moses, who was hitting the rock in the wilderness. "You shall strike the rock, and water shall come from it and the people will drink" (Exodus 17:6). Moses did as the Lord had commanded, and the rock produced water just as the Lord had said.

How could this rock produce water? What was the rock made of? Did it shoot straight up or just trickle like a drinking fountain? These are the questions I think of when I read this story. Paul told us in the New Testament about this very rock in the wilderness. He actually summed up the Israelites' journey from Egypt to where they were now, in the wilderness.

"For I do not want you to be unaware, brethren, that our fathers were all under the cloud and all passed through the sea; and all were baptized into Moses in the cloud and in the sea; and all ate the same spiritual food; and all drank the same spiritual drink, for *they were drinking from a spiritual rock which followed them; and the rock was Christ*" (1 Corinthians 10:1–4 NASB, emphasis added).

This rock apparently had *followed* them throughout their time in the wilderness. The word says it stayed with them wherever they went. We don't know whether it hopped along behind them or whether they picked it up and carried it; nonetheless, it was always with them all along their journey.

The end of verse 4 says this rock was Christ.

On Christ, the solid Rock, I stand;
All other ground is sinking sand. (Edward Mote)

What? Christ was with God's people all throughout their journey? He followed them wherever they went? This fact instantly makes me think about me being under the counter with Jesus. He was there all along, but I didn't know it at the time, just like the

Israelites didn't know the rock was Christ. I would have missed the blessing of knowing He was always with me and has never left me. As I write these words, even though I cannot see Jesus, I know He is right here with me, cheering me on and encouraging me to keep my focus on Him.

Let's go back to the woman at the well. She was literally standing next to the Christ, and He had just told her He had living water for her. Of course she says, "Give me this water, so that I will not be thirsty or have to come here to draw water" (John 4:15).

Jesus said something strange here. He said, "Okay, go get your husband and come here." She lied and told Him she didn't have a husband. Have you ever tried to lie to Jesus? I know I have, and the situation ends the same way it ended for her. He said, "I know you don't have one husband. You have had five, and you now are living with someone who is not your husband." Oops! She was busted. He knew all her secrets. There was no hiding from Him. Jesus just told her He was the awaited Messiah, meaning He was the one coming to save them. He was the one they had been waiting for, the Savior. He was the audience of One she had heard about her whole life.

After she found out who He was, He said to her, "They are ready. Go and tell the people in your village. The fields are white for harvest. What are you waiting for? Go and tell the people" (Trisha's translation).

Many Samaritans from that town believed in Him because of the woman's testimony (John 4:39).

Isn't that beautiful? Jesus ran into an unlikely woman, exposed her sin, gave her forgiveness, and offered her living, breathing, rushing water. Isn't that your story? I know that's mine. Jesus came, lived, died, and defeated death for me—*me*, the woman who had multiple husbands (not by this culture, but by biblical standards; sleeping with someone would constitute a marriage) and had lived to ignore You, God, most of my life. You came for me *so* I could live, *so* I could be free! *So* I could bare my shame and trade it for freedom. So I could kick out abandonment and welcome joy in all circumstances. He lavished me with order and discipline in my life *so* I could thrive. What? How can this be?

I wonder if that was what her testimony sounded like to the townspeople. She looked at everyone, saying, "Me, the woman you have shunned? The one who was left to draw water by myself in the heat of the day? Me! Do you see me, remember me? The one you judged for making shameful mistakes? The one who was so lonely and unseen that I disgraced myself with multiple men. Me! He gave *me* the water. *Me.* He looked at me in pure delight and said, 'GO walk on your dry ground and tell your people, about Me, your Jesus.'"

Her and my message is this: "Not only did He want me, but He wants you. Go and get your living water, walk on your dry ground. Free your soul for shame, guilt, bitterness, unforgiveness, and lay it at His feet. Jesus is waiting and looking at you in pure delight."

Lastly, the people of Samaria said to the woman, "It is no longer because of what you said that we believe, for we have heard for ourselves, and we know that this is indeed the Savior of the world" (4:42).

Again, my hope is that you have found yourself the Savior of the world. Go and dance on your dry ground for your audience of One. He is right there, delighting in you.

CHAPTER 17

The Kite Master

Faith is the art of holding on to things
in spite of your
changing moods and circumstances.

—C. S. Lewis

Why is it that the things I think I am exempt from, like fear or control, are the very things that entangle me? I would hear people struggling with either of these things and think, *Yeah, I just don't struggle with fear. It's just not my thing, or I don't really care about controlling things ... not my struggle.* Then I am slapped in the face with the fact that I have fears and control issues. What? I am genuinely surprised by this realization.

Now, on the other hand, I have always prided myself on how much faith I have. The it-will-all-work-out mentality is my go-to. But then bam!—I'm hit again with a season of doubt. I may not doubt God is God or that He knows best, but I doubt my freedom in Him. Isn't that the same thing? Isn't saying, "Lord I don't know if You can free me from this thing" the same thing as doubting God's goodness, mercy, or God-ness (if that is a word)?

"But he must ask with faith, without doubting, for the one who doubts is like the surf of the sea, driven and tossed by the waves" (James 1:6).

Rheanna Arfsten says in her book *Polished and Concealed,*

"Envision a kite that moves gracefully with the wind but is always controlled, because it is tethered to the keeper of its string. Now, picture the kite string breaking free. The kite is now moving with the wind: out of control, with no direction, being tossed by any and every gust that comes its way. It's chaos at best."

Chaos at best. That is how I feel in my season of doubting my freedom in Christ. Argh. No one wants to have chaos at *best*! Maybe chaos, at worst? Not chaos at best! Alas, that is where I land chaos … at best. These are the moments when I am on the floor of my closet with the door shut and lights off, crying out to the Lord to save me from myself.

It is as though I believe God has cut the kite string, like I am just floating along and minding my own business, swaying gently to and fro. Sure, I might have seconds or thirds on my lunch portion, or I might stay in bed and watch yet another Hallmark Christmas movie but nothing that *deserves* the severing of the cord. Right? But bam! It's cut (I think). I am on my own.

I better try harder! I better do more! Or I better do less, not be so overcommitted. Maybe I should quit something. Okay, I will call on that thing tomorrow and say I can't handle it anymore. That will solve it. Or, you know, now that I think about it, I think this is my husband's fault. Yeah, if he only helped me more and picked up some of the slack, then I could handle all this. He could do that on top of the business he runs, for sure! Right?

Tailspin.

What if? What if the Lord is just tightening up the slack between me and Him? What if He is drawing me in because I have been forgetting about His goodness a few too many times. What if He is calling me close to Him to remind me of His promises? What if it isn't a cutoff but a drawing near? As if He is whispering to me, "Daughter, don't try harder; trust Me, give it to Me. I can handle it. My yoke is easy. My burden is light. Hand it over. Let go. Let Me fly this thing. I've got it!"

This reminds me of the Israelites. After they had been walking with God for a while, they needed some tightening up *and* letting out of the line. This is what it looked like.

"On the third new moon after the people of Israel had gone out of the land of Egypt, on that day they came into the wilderness of Sinai" (Exodus 19:1).

Once they get settled into camp, God called Moses to the top of the mountain to tell him some things, actually a whole ton of things. God started with how much He desired the Israelites to be His chosen people, so he wanted to set them up to win.

The mountain was filled with God.

"Now when the people saw the thunder and the flashes of lightning and the sound of the trumpet and the mountain smoking, the people were afraid and trembled, and they stood far off and said to Moses, 'You speak to us, and we will listen; but do not let God speak to us, lest we die.' Moses said to the people, 'Do not fear, for God has come to test you, that the fear of him may be before you, that you may not sin.' The people stood far off, while Moses drew near to the thick darkness where God was" (Exodus 20:18–21).

The people drew back, and Moses drove in. The people said, "Ahh, this is too scary. I'm pulling back and waiting. We'll see how it turns out for Moses. Maybe I don't want to be tied to you. I will tie myself to Moses instead." How many times do I do that? *Oh, Lord, this all looks too scary. I think I will let the other lady do it instead. I will just follow what she says.* But not Moses. He said, "I'm coming in, Lord. Pull me tight to You and don't let go." And Moses went, and he learned all kinds of things from the Lord. God told him about the Law and how that was going to show the people their sin. It was going to work as a mirror to their souls. It would show the people their need for Him. God told Moses about slaves, restitution, sabbath, festivals, covenants, and the tabernacle. He learned what the priests should wear. I mean, they covered a lot of ground. All *for* the people. While Moses and God were doing all this work for the people, the Israelites weren't on the same page.

It's like this time when I was sitting on the couch, eating a grapefruit, and watching TV with my husband. I thought about how lucky I was to be married to him and wondered whether other wives felt like I did toward their husbands. I hoped so because it is such a wonderful thing to be head over heels for someone. Then suddenly Nate looked at me and said (I quote), "You are so annoying." Um, what? What did I do? What I didn't realize was that I wasn't exactly *eating* the grapefruit; apparently I was *slurping* it. Ha! That is marriage for you. We were on completely different planets of thinking.

We laugh about that story *now*. But that is kind of how it went down with Moses and the Israelites. Moses came down off the mountain with God to find the people melting down watches and bracelets to make a golden calf. They had taken their eyes off the goodness of God and went back to relying on their gods. Now before you think you are so much better than the Israelites, how many times have you taken your eyes off God and gone back to food, alcohol, gossip, Starbucks, shopping, approval of man— whatever your drug or golden calf of choice is? How many times have I? Too many to count.

All the while, I was thinking that God had given up on me and had cut the kite string. *You went too far this time, Trisha. I'm cutting you loose.*

Then I'm back in the spins. I'm flying all over the place.

What if the String Keeper is just letting out a bunch of string all at once? The kite goes flying around like crazy. It soars way up to new uncharted territories and reaches places it never dreamed of, all the while still tethered to the Kite Master.

That is me today. My Kite Master let out a bunch of string and let me soar. The flight was really scary at first, for sure. I had my doubts on what was happening. Did He cut the string? Am I lost now, with no control in sight? "For God has not given us the spirit of fear and timidity, but of power, love and a sound mind" (2 Timothy 1:7).

No chaos needed. I have power, love, and a sound mind *in the Spirit*! He has given me laws and rules to keep me safe and free, and He is available 24-7. A cloud by day and fire at night, guiding and leading me. Sometimes it sounds like thunder and looks like flashes of lightning, but I will draw in; You are the Thunder, the Lightning, my Kite Master. You are my "audience." You are my all.

CHAPTER 18

Pipe and Drape

No matter how much tarnish you think
is on the tabernacle of your heart,
you still shine because of God's love.

—Mark R. Woodward

This past year our church has been doing a satellite location at an elementary school. On the first day, our family showed up to learn how to set up the space and make it a church instead of a school for little people. The "Church on Wheels" people told us we would be learning how to put up "pipe and drape," which literally means pipes and drapes connected together, lining the walls and halls of the school to signify the correct space for the church.

Each week at the end of setup, no one would know it was a school because the pipe and drape transformed the space. It now was full of color; everything was clearly marked on where the sanctuary and children's ministry were. Some of the drapes are decorated with our names and mission statements. Some of them even had bright sunrises or twinkling lights for a selfie backdrop.

The pipe and drape didn't make the school a church, but it set up a space for us to *be* the church. When the Israelites were wandering in the wilderness, God gave them directions by a pillar of cloud by day and a pillar of fire by night. Then He told them to make Him a dwelling place, a tabernacle. That was a really "churchy" word.

Tab·er·nac·le; *noun*
1. (in biblical use) a fixed or movable habitation, typically of light construction.
2. a meeting place for worship [15]

"You shall make the tabernacle with ten curtains of fine-twined linen and blue and purple and scarlet yarns; you shall make them with cherubim skillfully worked into them" (Exodus 26:1),

Basically pipe and drape.

God gave the Israelites very specific directions on how to build the tabernacle. He wanted His dwelling place to be perfect. He wanted a place to rest and dwell. So every time the cloud moved, they broke down camp, moved the pipe and drape into the trailers, and hauled them to wherever the cloud or fire stopped. Then they set up camp again, and God dwelled in the tent.

This wasn't any ordinary tent with four walls and a leak in the side, so when you woke up, your pillow was drenched under your head. It wasn't a tent like that at all. It did have four fifteen-foot-high walls around the outside. The entire outer wall was fifty yards long by twenty-five yards wide. A big space! On the east side of the tabernacle was a ten-yard wide opening. Any one of the Israelites was welcome to enter the outer court or the courtyard of the tent. Before even entering the space, they would have been overcome by the smell.

The first thing one saw when walking through the gate was the bronze altar. This was where the sacrifice was made. The only way to atone for sin was sacrifice. The smell of burnt animals must have filled the air—not burnt like I burn *every* grilled cheese I

---

[15] https://www.dictionary.com

make but smoldering to the point that the only thing left of the lamb was smoke and ash.

Next to the bronze altar was the bronze laver, a washing station. After the sacrifice was made, they cleansed themselves. Only priests could enter the Holy Place; they would have to be clean—first clean of sin through sacrifice and then through a washing in the laver.

Inside the outer court or courtyard was another tent, fifteen by forty-five feet. The first section was the Holy Place. Inside the Holy Place were three things; one was the altar of incense, which held all prayers. Next was the shewbread; it contained twelve pieces of bread (replaced every week). Finally, was the lamp stand. The lamp stand lit the room and stood about five feet tall; it had seven candles (menorah).

Behind the altar of incense was a beautifully woven veil dividing the Holy Place from the Most Holy Place or the Holy of Holies. This was sacred ground. Once a year the high priest entered the Holy of Holies; this was where the presence of God was; this was His dwelling place. He would provide the only light so the high priest could see the ark of the covenant. Inside the ark was a jar of manna, Aaron's budded staff (Numbers 17–18), and the Ten Commandments (Exodus 20). The cover of the ark was the mercy seat (the atonement cover); this cover was extravagantly decorated with specific directions.

"And you shall make two cherubim of gold; of hammered work shall you make them, on the two ends of the mercy seat. Make one cherub on the one end, and one cherub on the other end. Of one piece with the mercy seat shall you make the cherubim on its two ends. The cherubim shall spread out their wings above, overshadowing the mercy seat with their wings, their faces one to another; toward the mercy seat shall the faces of the cherubim" (Exodus 25:18–20).

This blows my mind! They were in the wilderness and got these instructions to make this cover, the mercy seat for the Most

Holy Place. I want to meet the craftsmen who made this work of art for the God of the universe to have a place to dwell. That was an incredible task, an overwhelming calling. Why is this guy's name not in the Bible for all eternity? Thank you, unnamed guys, for using your amazing God-given talents for the glory of God.

The high priest entered under the veil to the Most Holy Place; by the way there was no door into this room. The priest had to crawl under the heavy veil (some say it was twelve inches wide) to enter God's presence. History states that his buddies tied a rope around him so if he died from being in the presence of God, they could drag out his dead body and not have to wait until next year to get him out.

The Holy of Holies was a sacred place, not to be messed with! Your life depended on it.

This temple wasn't just for the Israelites. "Or do you not know that your body is a temple of the Holy Spirit who is in you, whom you have from God, and that you are not your own?" (1 Corinthians 6:19).

The word *temple* is the same word as *tabernacle*. Our bodies are God's tabernacle, His dwelling place. The place He perfectly designed. The tabernacle in its entirety is an amazingly beautiful picture for us. Admittedly when I first knew I would have to study the tabernacle, I didn't jump out of my seat to do it. The topic sounded extremely boring and unimportant. But what I found out was that neither of those things was true. Now that you have taken the time to get a bird's eye view of the space, let me break down what it all means to us.

Bronze Altar	Jesus is the sacrifice for our sins.
Bronze Laver	We are baptized into Christ Jesus.
Shewbread	God provides.
Lamp Stand	Jesus is the Light of the world.
Altar of Incense	God hears our prayers (Revelation 8:3–4).

Jar of Manna	God creates something from nothing.
Budded Staff	God is a God of miracles.
Ten Commandments	God is a God of order and discipline.
Mercy Seat	Jesus has atoned for all sin. His mercy is new every morning.

First, as a whole the temple or tabernacle is us. As believers and followers of Christ, our bodies are a living temple of God. All these things are true. Jesus died for your sins. You are cleansed by His blood. He provides for your every need. He lights your path with Himself. He hears your prayers. He will create something from nothing. He performs miracles. He is order and disciple, and He atoned for *all*. He covered all sin and has mercy on you.

Every square inch of our temple is accounted for, every nano particle of my body planned ahead for a purpose and a calling to glorify God. "For you formed my inward parts; you knitted me together in my mother's womb" (Psalm 130:13).

As you can imagine, as a woman, this concept is a struggle for me. You made me this way? This is Your perfect vessel to dwell in? Why is it that I cannot see that I am perfectly made? I look at pictures of me and think I am flawed somehow? A friend of mine said she was a reverse of anorexia. People who suffer from anorexia look in the mirror and hate themselves. The reverse anorexic looks in the mirror and thinks she looks pretty good. Then someone shows her a picture of herself, and shock comes. *What? That is what I look like?* She thinks. This is exactly what happens to me. I look in the mirror and think, *Girl, you look good.* But the minute a picture is taken, horror sets in. Why is that? Do my eyes lie to me? Does a photograph tell me my worth? Did it create me? Does it get to tell me who I am?

The computer I am typing on right now started having issues. The left shift key stopped working. I tried to fix it myself by restarting the computer; that's where my expertise starts and stops. So then when that didn't work, I called a friend of mine, who is "computer savvy"; he tried to help but to no avail. Then I drove to a fix-it shop and tried to get them to fix the problem. They told me I needed to go to the creator of the computer, and they were the only ones able to fix the key. So as a last resort, I got in the car and drove to the Apple store forty-five minutes away from my house; there I talked to the creator of my computer. It was my last resort but the best and only real option. They fixed the key fast and for free.

That is how God works. He is the Creator of my body and is ready and waiting for me to turn my focus to Him and ask Him who I am. I can ask Him to fix any keys that are stuck or thinking that is off. He is ready to show me the truth free of charge.

Because of disobedience, Moses never walked to the promised land, but He saw it. He led many others to the promised land. So do you think Moses's mission failed because he didn't live in the promised land? What if the mission was in the middle? What if success was in the discipline? What if where you thrive and grow and show others the promised land *is* the goal? What if the goal isn't 130 pounds? What if it's taking care of this body as a living temple? What if it's loving our kids right where they are, not wishing we had more time for ourselves one day? Or maybe peace in the growing is the goal, not the arrival. Success is in the middle of your day-to-day life, staying still in the Lord, praying for the chaos of the world without being of it, and being ready to go when He says, "Go, walk on your dry land."

Audience of One: Testimonies

> They triumphed over him by the blood of the Lamb and
> by the word of their testimony.
> —Revelation 12:11

This whole concept of living for an audience of One is a lifelong process. I have given you some good examples and some not-so-good examples of what it looks like to live for God alone.

This morning I woke up with a song playing in my head. "It may look like I'm surrounded, but I'm surrounded by You"[16] played over and over.

I am at the point in this process where I am asking people to read this book and give me feedback or testimonies. Argh, the fear of man comes crashing in like waves from nowhere. I have to keep reminding myself that this book exists because God was with me every step of the way. He told me when to write and when to take a break. I went for weeks and had no desire to write anything. Then bam! My fingers wouldn't work fast enough to type the concepts He showed me. The process was glorious.

So even though I *feel* like I'm surrounded, I *know* I'm surrounded by You, Lord!

I met one of my very best friends right after I accepted Christ. Nate and I were able to scrape together some money and build the

---

[16] Michael W. Smith, Surrounded.

house we are in now, like I told you before. But what I didn't say is that I was still really wounded from losing my BFF Nicole, so when I met Amber across the street, my only prayer was, "Don't let me be the crazy God lady!" It was one of those friendships. I knew immediately that we would be great friends, so I really didn't want to mess it up with my love for Jesus.

God was so clear with me that this was going to be a great friend of mine that when we bought a house on the other side of the neighborhood, I had no peace. I told Nate, "I just really think we need to be on the other end." I didn't tell him it was because I thought we should be by the family we had just met while driving by. That would have been crazy. But that was the reason.

My plan was just to keep God in my pocket so this woman would like me. Well, God had another plan.

Our kids shared a bus stop at Amber's house, so I had a great excuse to talk with her in the mornings and afternoons. Soon we moved into the kitchen for "coffee talks." Every time I was at her house, she brought up God *and* asked really hard questions. For example: "What about the person on the deserted island who was never told about God or given a Bible? Are you saying they will go to hell? Or what about the person who doesn't have the mental capacity to choose Jesus? You're saying hell?" I answered if I felt like I had an answer or just said, "I don't know. That's a great question, but I do know God is good." Then I left and got mad at myself for talking about God so much. *Argh, Trisha, you did it again.*

Without my knowing, God had her praying she would find a neighbor or friend with whom to sit on the porch and have coffee. Her faith was very religious and full of the dos and don'ts, not a relationship. So my "relational faith" was fascinating to her; she wanted to know more.

Eventually, I asked her to go to a Bible study with me. She missed the first week, so of course I figured this was a fail, but the second week she came. During the video I felt God nudging me to pray with her. *Um, no. Remember, Lord, I don't want to be the crazy God lady who will scare her away.* But I did it anyway. I prayed, and she starting crying.

It turns out that the talks we had, a book I gave her, and the Bible study all led her to this moment when she decided to give her life over fully to the Lord. That's not even true. I wasn't the one who led her to Christ. Jesus walked alongside both of us and left us bread crumbs to follow and draw us near to Him. He was the driving force on all sides. We may not have been living for an audience of One, but He was still there, ready for the moment we turned and trusted Him.

It turns out that being the crazy God lady is what drew her in, and now we aren't just friends but sisters in Christ. Praise God! Amber texted me later that day and said, "I think God has a sense of humor because as you were praying, I really wanted to climb onto your lap and snuggle you." Then she laughed and said, "He would know we would think that was funny." I don't think that was it all in this case, although God is *really* funny. I believe she saw Jesus in this flawed girl and wanted to snuggle with her Savior.

Even if we don't get it right, even if we fight Him all the way, as long as we keep talking to Him and asking questions, He will give us the courage to live for Him alone.

I have asked a few of the people I admire and walk with every day to share what living for God alone has looked like for them. Here are their stories.

I struggle with focusing on an audience-of-one mind-set. I think it's mostly because I care too much about what other people think of me. In the past, I even tweaked my personality to the people I was with to make sure what I did and said fit in with how I thought they wanted me to be. In doing that, I had lost myself.

As I began to find Jesus, I also began finding myself. As I spent quiet time reading about God and praying, I caught glimpses of the real me. I wasn't being fake. The more time I spent doing this, the more of myself I was finding. I started doing and saying things that came from my relationship with Jesus, not from my need to please others.

This has taken a huge weight off my shoulders. When I feel the need to perform for the world, my anxiety kicks back in. When I focus on performing for my audience of One, I feel I'm exactly who I was meant to be.

—Nicole Nelson, author of *Cursed with Common Sense*

The concept of living for an audience of One isn't an easy one for me to embrace. Not because I don't understand it or disagree with its importance but because I am so often drawn toward worldly things. I like comfort, familiarity, staying under the radar, not rocking the boat; and I fear being rejected or not fitting in. I admit that I spend so much of my time living for the approval of others, even those I hardly know. And if I really think about it, it seems so strange that I put that much time and effort into something that gives me such a low level, fleeting satisfaction.

When I look at the times in my life when I've felt the most happiness, joy, rushes of excitement, and feelings of peace, those were the times where I felt a calling from God and obeyed. Times when He stretched me out of my comfort zone and asked me to do something for Him or with Him. These were times when I decided not to care about what others thought and put myself out there where God asked me to go. There's a rush, an excitement of doing things that you know are not your idea, because it's the last thing you would choose if it was up to you. There's an almost electric connection between you and God when you know you are choosing to be obedient and giving yourself over to Him and

His will for you and your life. Every time He has asked me to do something, like reach out to a stranger or acquaintance, for example (and I've chosen to say yes and live for Him), I have been blessed in amazing ways. I've felt the rush of being part of His "team" and working for the kingdom of God. I've felt that electric connection, that amazing high, and I have fallen in love with Him and His greatness and glory all over again.

His love is amazing, His gifts are amazing, His grace is amazing, His mercy is amazing. The fact that the God of all things wants a personal give-and-take relationship with us is amazing. It is also overwhelming and wonderful and beautiful, and when we choose to live for an audience of One, we get to fully experience all these blessings. It isn't an easy thing to do. I am not an expert at it, and I continually struggle with it. But when we are able to let go of ourselves and live for Him, it is so, so worth it!

—Amber Olson, BFF, wife, boy mom,
gracious and merciful sister-in-Christ

Putting into words what my heart feels when I think of living for God and God alone almost feels impossible, partly because I would have to share my life story in full for you to understand how I have gotten where I am and partly because I know I still haven't fully figured it out. What I know is that at one point in my life, I lived for an audience of all the humans around me, almost not even thinking about God. These years left me feeling anxious, sad, scared, worthless, hopeless, and purposeless. The journey He has allowed me to take in discovering the joy, hope, and complete peace that comes with living for Him and Him alone has been equal parts painful, exhilarating, confusing, and freeing. It's always painful and confusing to let go of the ugly need to please others. But it's worth it to get to the point of the pure joy of serving God alone. The more I think of *only* God when it comes to how I live my life, the more confidence, hope, joy, and freedom I experience. The more I allow my life to be dedicated to serving, loving, and living for my Creator, the more I know I will never purposely live for anyone else ever again except for my audience of One.

—Melissa Schaefer, author of *All Touched Out*

Living for an audience of One for me looks like reckless freedom. Freedom from the opinions of others, freedom from needing to please *every single* person in your life, freedom to be the person God made you to be and not doubt for a second His extraordinary love for you. I wish I could say that I live in this reality, but the truth is, it's a daily struggle for me. I've strived for love my entire life by trying to perform at an impossible standard that no one ever asked me to perform at; these standards were all created by me. This obviously overflowed into my relationship with God, and as I found myself constantly attending Bible studies, reading self-help books, leading ministries, serving, and so forth, I was thinking that I needed to do these things to please my heavenly Father. It wasn't until I truly grasped the reality that it was complete foolishness to think that I could do something to earn God's love that my perspective began to change. Isaiah talks about righteous deeds creating nothing more than filthy rags. Did you know that the literal translation means used menstrual garments? Yuck! So there I was, offering up my used maxi pads, thinking, *Now God will surely love me!* How foolish of me! As you can imagine, this left me exhausted and overwhelmed all too often, and I would come, crying to God, begging for answers of why my burden felt so heavy and why I had such little joy. Each time I would do this, He would whisper, "Heather, you cannot earn my love. It is a gift. You just need to receive it and stop trying so hard."

I think all too often we approach God the same as we do the other relationships in our lives. We mistakenly think that if we really showed our true self, didn't "perform" well enough, or simply were honest about what was going on within us, He would be disappointed or, worse, abandon us. Thank You, Jesus, that this isn't the way You operate. Our salvation isn't a result of our special abilities, sacrifices, or lists of things we do for God; rather, it is that once we receive the love so freely offered to us, with no strings attached, these things will come naturally because of the gratitude we have for our salvation. We have the greatest promise that anyone could ever have, and that is eternal love. Love that will never go away no matter what we do or don't do. This is what should usher us into that reckless freedom. So be free, be you, be undone by His love, and live for your audience of One.

—Heather Norgren, marriage coach, wife,
mother, and warrior for Christ

Afterword

Be strong and courageous.
Do not be frightened, and do not be dismayed,
for the Lord your God is with you
wherever you go.

—Joshua 1:9 ESV

I'm finishing with this story in Psalm 78 (MSG). This summarizes the Israelites' walk with their God and their constant rebellion. How would their lives have been different if they had kept their eyes on their audience of One?

> Listen, dear friends, to God's truth, bend your ears to what I tell you. I'm chewing on the morsel of a proverb; I'll let you in on the sweet old truths, stories we heard from our fathers, counsel we learned at our mother's knee.
>
> We're not keeping this to ourselves, we're passing it along to the next generation—God's fame and fortune, the marvelous things he has done.
>
> He planted a witness in Jacob, set his Word firmly in Israel, then commanded our parents to teach it to their children so the next generation would know, and all the generations to

come—know the truth and tell the stories so their children can trust in God, never forget the works of God, but keep his commands to the letter.

Heaven forbid they should be like their parents, bullheaded and bad, a fickle and faithless bunch who never stayed true to God.

The Ephraimites, armed to the teeth, ran off when the battle began. They were cowards to God's Covenant, refused to walk by his Word. They forgot what he had done—marvels he'd done right before their eyes.

He performed miracles in plain sight of their parents in Egypt, out on the fields of Zoan.

He split the Sea and they walked right through it; he piled the waters to the right and the left. He led them by day with a cloud, led them all night long with a fiery torch. He split rocks in the wilderness, gave them all they could drink from underground springs; He made creeks flow out from sheer rock, and water poured out like a river.

All they did was sin even more, rebel in the desert against the High God. They tried to get their own way with God, clamored for favors, for special attention. They whined like spoiled children, "Why can't God give us a decent meal in this desert? Sure, he struck the rock and the water flowed, creeks cascaded from the rock. But how about some fresh-baked bread? How about a nice cut of meat?"

When God heard that, he was furious—his anger flared against Jacob, he lost his temper with Israel. It was clear they didn't believe in God, had no intention of trusting in his help. But God helped them anyway, commanded the clouds and gave orders that opened the gates of heaven.

He rained down showers of manna to eat, he gave them the Bread of Heaven. They ate the bread of the mighty angels; he sent them all the food they could eat. He let East Wind break loose from the skies, gave a strong push to South Wind.

This time it was birds that rained down—succulent birds, an abundance of birds. He aimed them right for the center of their camp; all round their tents there were birds. They ate and had their fill; he handed them everything they craved on a platter.

But their greed knew no bounds; they stuffed their mouths with more and more. Finally, God was fed up, his anger erupted—he cut down their brightest and best, he laid low Israel's finest young men.

And—can you believe it?—they kept right on sinning; all those wonders and they still wouldn't believe! So their lives dribbled off to nothing—nothing to show for their lives but a ghost town.

When he cut them down, they came running for help; they turned and pled for mercy. They gave witness that God was their rock, that High God was their redeemer, but they didn't mean a word of it; they lied through their teeth the whole time. They could not have cared less about him, wanted nothing to do with his Covenant.

And God? Compassionate! Forgave the sin! Didn't destroy! Over and over he reined in his anger, restrained his considerable wrath. He knew what they were made of; he knew there wasn't much to them. How often in the desert they had spurned him, tried his patience in those wilderness years. Time and again they pushed him to the limit, provoked Israel's Holy God. How quickly they forgot what he'd done, forgot their day of rescue from the enemy, when he did miracles in Egypt, wonders on the plain of Zoan.

He turned the River and its streams to blood—not a drop of water fit to drink. He sent flies, which ate them alive, and frogs, which bedeviled them. He turned their harvest over to caterpillars, everything they had worked for to the locusts.

He flattened their grapevines with hail; a killing frost ruined their orchards. He pounded their cattle with hail, let thunderbolts loose on their herds. His anger flared, a wild firestorm of havoc, an advance guard of disease-carrying angels to clear the ground, preparing the way before him. He didn't spare those people, he let the plague rage through their lives. He killed all the Egyptian firstborns, lusty infants, offspring of Ham's virility. Then he led his people out like sheep, took his flock safely through the wilderness. He took good care of them; they had nothing to fear. The Sea took care of their enemies for good.

He brought them into his holy land, this mountain he claimed for his own. He scattered everyone who got in their way; he staked out an inheritance for them—the tribes of Israel all had their own places.

I pray that you are abundantly blessed by reading my story. I pray you will see Christ all around your life and in your circumstances. I pray you will know that your audience is *singular*. It isn't the masses. The masses are most often all lost and trying harder than you to find purpose and direction, all the while climbing over one another to do so. The real person who matters is Christ alone. He is your "audient," your audience of One, and He is there with you *now*, delighting in you. Keep your eyes fixed on *the* Audience of One.

About the Author

This has been a growing and stretching process for me as well as my family. My children and husband have sacrificed their time with me time and time again so I could learn the writing process in an attempt to do this well. This is the first of what I hope to be many books or Bible studies in the future.

This isn't what I expected my life to look like, but I am in love. I love being a mom. I love homeschooling the kids, even on days like today when my son asks whether he can go to school. I don't know whether homeschool is forever. I just want to do what God has for our family, even if we can't see the fruit right now.

I never expected to be a house wife, but I cannot imagine not being married to this man of mine. He is often referred to as my "Moon and My Stars." I really do adore him, and he is also gracious enough to take the back seat to our Lord and Savior. Praise Jesus.

Author was never, ever on my to-do list, but now that I am here, I don't want to stop. Jesus is a wild ride, and I don't plan to get off. My audience is watching and waiting for me to take the next leap. I can't wait to hear what's next. Right now I will be still.

Notes

Notes

Notes

Notes